HAUNTINGS,
POSSESSIONS,
AND EXORCISMS

HAUNTINGS, POSSESSIONS, AND EXORCISMS

ADAM C. BLAI

EMMAUS ROAD PUBLISHING

Steubenville, Ohio
www.EmmausRoad.org

Emmaus Road Publishing
1468 Parkview Circle
Steubenville, Ohio 43952

Library of Congress Cataloging-in-Publication Data
Names: Blai, Adam C., 1970- author.
Title: Hauntings, possessions, exorcisms / Adam C. Blai.
Description: Steubenville : Emmaus Road Pub, 2017.
Identifiers: LCCN 2017031015 (print) | LCCN 2017031534 (ebook) | ISBN
    9781945125607 (ebook) | ISBN 9781945125591 (pbk.)
Subjects: LCSH: Demonology. | Exorcism. | Spiritual warfare. | Catholic
    Church--Doctrines.
Classification: LCC BX2340 (ebook) | LCC BX2340 .B53 2017 (print) | DDC
    264/.020994--dc23
LC record available at https://lccn.loc.gov/2017031015

Cover image: *Temptation on the Mount* (ca. 1308–11)
by Duccio di Buoninsegna, The Frick Collection, New York City.

Cover design and layout by Margaret Ryland

This book is dedicated to my friends in the exorcist community.
You know who you are.

✝

CONTENTS

†

PROLOGUE

"LORD, HAVE MERCY ON US," the exorcist intoned, starting the litany of the saints that precedes an exorcism. "Christ, have mercy on us," he said as we held onto the woman, waiting for the demon to take over as it became enraged by the prayers. I took a moment to reflect as I sat beside her, my arms tightly wrapped around her left arm. We ask for mercy so many times at the beginning of the exorcism, but, I wondered, why? "Lord, have mercy on us," the exorcist continued. And then the woman went limp. "Christ, hear us," he prayed, somewhat louder now. Something was happening inside the woman's body. I thought I felt quivers, a tension. I checked to be sure she couldn't get a grip on my flesh or fingers and that she couldn't reach me with her teeth.

"Christ, graciously hear us," he said as a small curl of a smile crept around her mouth. A second later her eyes shot open and she lunged off the couch, leering with a wide feral smile, hissing and growling at the priest, straining her hands to reach him. She thrashed from side to side a bit and wrenched away from me and the others who were trying to restrain her. We pulled her back down to a safe sitting position on the couch. She cocked her head and glared with hate at the exorcist, suddenly calm but for her hissing.

The woman's face relaxed as the demon turned slowly toward me. Casually it said, "You seem a little shaky today." I looked it in the eye for a moment and refocused on my job: gently restraining this one arm. Something about that comment unsettled me deeply.

The demon smiled as I looked down and waited for the next response to give to the litany. It slowly turned back to the priest and, baring its teeth, leaned forward as far as it could, trying to bite him as it lifted the three of us off the couch. This was a difficult case and had been going on for years, and I had only joined in on the past year's worth of exorcisms for this particular case.

Later that night the unsettling comment began to make sense to me: We've become familiar with each other. I've assisted at so many exorcisms the demons were making small talk. They had become familiar enough that I could often tell when we were dealing with a certain demon or whether it was a totally new creature. I had become so used to being around possessed people that these strange and violent scenes seemed normal. But I also knew that demons will do anything to get in someone's head, to shake someone up. They try to terrorize everyone present if they can, scanning the room to take the measure of each person present before attacking the weakest.

Despite general trends and current opinions, the Catholic Church has always maintained that Satan and his fallen angels are real. They are personal beings and not just a privation of good or merely the evil in people's hearts. Demons are fallen angels who were cast down to earth, not hell, to roam here until the final judgment (see Rev 12:8). They were never human. They are allowed to tempt humans as their normal activity, which means people must exercise free will to interact with them.

I have been involved in assisting the Church's efforts in demonic and human spirit cases for over ten years, including dozens of solemn exorcisms. I'm involved in training priests nationally to do exorcisms and I consult on cases for a number of dioceses. I have been given the title Peritus of Religious Demonology and Exorcism by decree of my bishop.

Unfortunately, my work and the work of others is necessary in a world that is decreasingly religious and has lain down the sword of spiritual combat in all but a small number of contexts. However, the battle the Church continues to wage is dependent on that which my mind kept turning to before the demon's disturbing comment: Mercy.

Mercy is at the heart of deliverance ministry and exorcisms, on which this book is intended to provide a Catholic perspective. This is not a how-to book for working on demonic cases but an introduction to the subject. My hope is that you will come away with knowledge that will help you avoid spiritual problems, as well as an understanding of how cases are resolved. This book, however, does not make one qualified to deal with the demonic.

As we pray for any exorcism, we beg for mercy—partly because we choose to fight an enemy we cannot really understand. We beg for mercy because it is only God who can restrain and limit the demon's strength and keep us alive. We beg for mercy so that our spiritual vulnerabilities will be protected from the attack of the enemy, so that our minds will be protected from the insanity that has claimed some in the past. We beg for mercy because, in this spiritual warfare, we know and are known.

PART I

✝

✝

GENERAL CONSIDERATIONS

INTRODUCTION

JESUS WAS VERY CLEAR about the reality of the Devil. He exorcised demons in seven major Gospel accounts. He differentiated between healings of natural illness, healings of the effects of sin, and the casting out of demons. He empowered and explicitly charged His disciples to cast out demons as part of their mission before He ascended to heaven (see Mk 16:17). The Church responded to His command and performed many exorcisms from the very beginning of Christianity onward. For more about exorcism in Scripture and our biblical understanding of demons, see Appendix I: Some Lessons from the Bible. For now, it suffices to say that exorcism was an integral part of baptism into the early Church. Oftentimes these early exorcisms were done by lay people, but in the following centuries, after much experience, the Church wisely limited the ministry to select priests with proper traits and training.

In 1986 Pope John Paul II gave a talk in which he reminded the faithful about the dangers of the Devil. Not long after, in 1990, a small group of priests formed the International Association of Exorcists. This group, which

3

has grown each year, provides training to priests appointed by their bishops, as well as a handful of lay people. More recently, the USCCB held a conference on exorcism and published questions and answers about the subject on their website.

While the Church has been responding to the Holy Spirit and relearning how to combat evil spirits, the world has also been rediscovering spirits—but in a different way. A new spiritualist movement has exploded in the United States, as well as many other countries, with the help of every form of media. This has normalized interest and interaction with evil spirits. Meanwhile, ignorance of the dangers of the spiritual world abounds. Thousands of people participate in "paranormal investigation groups" and seek out spiritual manifestations and communication. Although these activities have been popularized in television and movies, they are anything but harmless forms of entertainment. In reality, many of the demonic cases the Church handles occur as a result of these practices. Unfortunately, most people believe without a doubt the misinformation supplied by the entertainment business, which by nature is more interested in selling sensationalism than sober truth. A correct view of these matters requires an understanding of certain basic principles.

FUNDAMENTAL CONCEPTS AND SUMMARY STATEMENTS

Many people have ideas about the spiritual world and demons based on movies, television, or popular books. In order to form a correct and effective perspective one needs to understand:

- Demons are fallen angels who God cast down to earth to roam here until the final judgment (Rev 12:8). They are not, nor were they ever human. They tempt people as their regular activity, which provides the opportunity for humans to exercise free will.
- **The spiritual world is legalistic.** There are rules that spirits operate under; these rules were created by God.
- **God is always present and always in charge of what spirits are allowed to do.** Demons are not running loose, free to do whatever they want.
- **Human spirits in Purgatory generally only communicate a need for prayer, or a need for help with unfinished restitution of a sin.** There are rare exceptions to this but generally if there is ongoing dialogue it is not with a human spirit.
- **Demons are limited to whatever legal rights people have given them by their free will choices.** Since God does not violate people's free will, they can choose to form a relationship with demons, even if they are baptized Christians. Once legal rights have been given to demons, those rights must be removed before the demons can be cast away.
- The free will choices of **parents for their children** can give legal rights for interaction. The good version of this is baptism; the bad version is when parents consecrate their children to the enemy. The free will choices of **ancestors for their family line** can give legal rights for interaction. Legal rights in these cases can be renounced by the current gener-

ation on behalf of the one that caused the problem in the past.

- **Spiritual problems are corrective experiences allowed by God.** They serve to educate and correct us, like correcting a child's understanding so they do not get hurt again. This is why cases sometimes linger until the people change their lives and grow closer to God in their behavior and hearts.

The following are some summary statements that should address common questions and clarify expectations:

- **There are five types of spiritual cases:** souls in purgatory signaling a need for prayer (hauntings), demons pretending to be human souls, demonic infestations of places, demonic oppression of people, and demonic possession of people. Exceptions to these types of cases occur, but are rare.
- **There are only six types of spiritual being besides God:** holy angels, saints, living human souls, souls in purgatory, fallen angels, and damned souls. There are no other types of spirits, but demons will masquerade as whatever type of spirit will engender interaction.
- **The way to resolve a human spirit haunting is to pray for the dead, preferably in the form of the Mass.** This means asking forgiveness for their sins and offering up prayers for the remission of the temporal punishment for their sins. Talking to the dead doesn't help, is forbidden in the Bible, and generally leads to problems.
- **There is no "magic wand" to deal with demonic problems.** People often want a quick fix without

doing any work or changing their lives. This doesn't happen because the legal rights the demons have usually involve the life and choices of the person being afflicted.

- In rare cases a "curse" is the cause of spiritual problems. A "curse" is simply a demon sent to harm a person. They generally have no effect on people obedient to God's rules and living a proper sacramental life.

- Demonic infestations should be addressed by trained clergy as they often involve house exorcisms.

- Demonic oppression is best addressed through correcting the spiritual life and fully participating in the sacraments. Deliverance prayer is sometimes needed after the spiritual life is corrected.

- Demonic possession is when the demon has gained the right to take over the body. The demon may be "in" the body but unable to take it over before this point. Being "in" the body is not the same as possession. Possession is treated with solemn exorcism, which can only be done by a priest with the permission of his bishop.

MEDICAL AND MENTAL ILLNESS

The great majority of demonic complaints from people are based on misunderstandings, medical illness, or mental illness. Some cases involve a combination of genuine spiritual problems and medical or mental illness, and most genuine demonic cases show at least some disturbance in the emotions or thought processes. Some cases are clearly based on a spiritual problem and there is little normal distress in the person or their lives, as is seen mostly in cases of full possession of a devout Catholic with a supportive family.

Some of the common misunderstandings, medical illnesses, and mental illnesses attributed to demons are:

- **Sleep disorders.** These disorders account for most complaints of negative spiritual activity. Always be aware of problems that only occur when tired, going to sleep, or waking.
    - Hypnopompic and hypnagogic hallucinations: When moving into sleep (hypnopompic) or out of sleep (hypnagogic), people pass through a state of consciousness where they may dream while partly awake. They are not aware that they are dreaming and so these experiences seem real.
    - Sleep paralysis: This is a malfunction of the natural immobilization of the body during sleep. It leads to a condition where someone is partly awake, is paralyzed from the eyes down, and sees things. It is a very frightening experience in which the person can look around but cannot scream or move their body. The website www.nightterrors.org can be a helpful resource in understanding sleep paralysis.
- **Hysteria.** This is fear accentuated by other people. With the popularity of paranormal television shows and movies, it is not uncommon to find people that are hypersensitized to sounds or temperature changes due to a fear of ghosts. In some cases, parents can encourage this fear in their young children who then subconsciously accept these ideas.

- **Hormones.** It is common that women in older age experience strange body sensations caused by hormone changes. When this is combined with early-onset dementia or general mental decline, the person may become fixated on a demonic hypothesis to explain their experiences.
- **Drugs.** There are many mental issues that can arise from the use of, or withdrawal from, street drugs. It is also not uncommon for older people to make errors in taking their medications and have psychosis as a side effect of this.
- **Brain disease.** There are many disorders and diseases that can affect the brain, causing psychotic experiences (a break from reality). A spiritual complaint could be based on the onset of schizophrenia, depression or manic-depression with psychotic symptoms, a brain tumor, or epilepsy, for instance. There are several other brain-based problems that can cause false experiences and paranoid fears.
- **Head or spine injuries.** It is not uncommon to encounter people who have had a head or spine injury and attribute their pains and sensations to spiritual attacks. There can be a psychotic aspect to these cases when the person is very resistant to any other hypothesis about their symptoms, no matter how reasonable.
- **Malingering.** Malingering is when a person pretends to be sick in order to get attention. Some people see the special attention people get on television shows and so use complaints about spirits to become the center of attention. This sometimes happens with young children who are neglected.

- **Factitious disorders.** A factitious disorder is when a person pretends to be sick for a practical gain. These situations are rare. In one case the false story of ghost molestations was used by a sex offender to cover up the crimes in their home. In another case a person wanted to use demonic influence as an excuse to avoid conviction for a gun crime.
- **Ocular misperceptions.** At the edge of the retina there is only black and white vision and little detail. Since the nervous system does not work perfectly at all times, this leads to the occasional perception of a black and white vague shadow at the edge of vision. When the person turns to look, bringing the full detailed color vision at the middle of the retina to bear, the "shadow" disappears.

Sometimes people blame regular life problems or mental illness on curses or demonic activity. This externalizes problems for the person. They often read extensively about possession and exorcism, both online and in books, and self-diagnose their problems. These cases can take on a sad desperation where the person goes from diocese to diocese demanding an exorcism based on their self-diagnosis, refusing any other hypothesis. Exorcism is reserved for cases of full possession only. If there is a curse on the person, the sacramental life and deliverance prayers should resolve it.

Some complaints are genuine spiritual problems along with medical or mental issues. These problems can be unrelated or secondary to the spiritual problem. It is typical for people living in infested homes to get very little sleep and spend their time at home in great anxiety. This often leads to irritability and mild depression. It is also common with oppression and possession for people to develop medical problems secondary to the spiritual affliction.

Every case is unique and there is no simple way to discern all of these possibilities. Getting a medical and mental checkup is an essential step if there is any doubt. Leaving a medical or mental illness untreated because a person feels their issues are being addressed by the Church can be irresponsible and lead to harm through neglect. Having the person under some medical supervision while spiritual issues are addressed is the best course of action in cases of possession.

†

DEMONIC CON GAMES:
THE NATURE AND BEHAVIOR
OF DEMONS

GIVEN THEIR NEED to get the free-will permission for each step of the process, a demon must play games with a targeted person. These games are tailored specifically to that person's needs and weaknesses. In the beginning the demons may feign weakness and neediness or pretend that their target has power over them. In other cases, they may offer power or some form of short term success (a "deal with the Devil"). Sometimes they offer what seems to be psychic information about the future. When people are abused or neglected as children the demons may offer companionship or the power of protection, which the person may grow to rely on over the years. In this section we'll go over some of the common con games that demons play in order to gain access into a person's life.

RULES THAT DEMONS OPERATE UNDER

The spiritual world is legalistic—meaning there are "rules" or spiritual realities that spiritual beings operate under.

Before we talk about the rules, it helps to know what a demon actually is.

Demons were initially created as holy angels with free will, but were given the choice whether to serve God or not. When they chose to follow Satan, they were greatly diminished and deformed as they were cast away from God down to earth. They retain vestiges of the powers they were created with—each angel has a unique function and faculties to perform that function. They are now permanently separated from God and under the direction of Satan, living in a hierarchical army based solely on fear, torture, and self-hatred. However, somewhat ironically, we know that demons are in fact subservient creatures of God. We see this in both the Old Testament with Job and the New Testament when the demons recognize, obey, and make requests of Jesus as one with authority over them. This is true in exorcisms today where we see that demons are under the control of the head exorcist, Jesus Christ.

The basic rules that demons operate under are: (1) Demons can't do anything extraordinary without at least initial permission—they require an act of free will. While temptation is their ordinary action, God allows their extraordinary actions; (2) Demons are allowed to use deception in order to gain rights over a person; and (3) Demons will not stop interfering with a person or space until told to leave explicitly by the authority of God through the ministry of the Church. Let's look at those more closely.

1) Demons can't do anything extraordinary without at least initial permission—they require an act of free will.

Because the rules of the spiritual world were created by God, He is always present and enforcing what spirits can and cannot do. God does not wish the demons to afflict humans, but His perfect justice allows it to a point. God allows this short-term, corrective pain because He will not violate our free will and force us to turn away from the demons. Therefore, He does not violate the free will of anyone who chooses to form a relationship with demons, even if they are baptized Christians. Of course, the hope remains that when people experience the ugly truth of a relationship with Satan they will come back to God's loving protection.

Demons claim rights to act based on the free-will choices of the people with authority over what the demons want—whether it be a building, or a body, or even an individual's ancestor. When a child is not of age to make free will choices, their parents have spiritual authority to make choices for them. Take for example Baptism, where God honors the spiritual choice of the parents for the baby that cannot yet choose the sacrament. Some parents willingly give their children to demonic powers when they are still in the womb or shortly after birth. This can be done in a multi-generational cult or some other circumstance where a person has authority over a child.

When the demon encounters a person who is intervening in the case, they are likewise bound by that person's choices.

2) Demons are allowed to use deception in order to gain rights over a person. This can include, but is not limited to pretending to be a human spirit, communicating kindly before becoming malevolent, promising power or material things before turning against a person, and other tricks. They can be attached to people and families (obsession, possession); physical spaces (infestation); and objects (curses).

The process of possession plays out as the person's relationship with the demon deepens step-by-step. The afflictions and control increase as the demon gains more rights. Early on the demon often pretends to be helpful, like a friend. When the demon or demons have enough rights to be confident that the person can't cast them away on their own, they become mean and controlling. Later, when their rights are extensive, a demon may torture the person so severely that they agree to give over use of their body in exchange for the torture to stop. Charismatic cult leaders employ the same tactics: they shower people with love and affirmation, gradually demand that their followers renounce their liberties and property, and then eventually dominate their lives completely with fear.

Demons may try to goad the person into overstepping their boundaries or acting in their own names. They sometimes try to get the person to sacrifice themselves under the delusion that taking the demon into themselves will free the person. This results in two victims because the rights over the body are still held by Satan, and if the body has many demons in it, a few can be sent into the body of the new person without helping the victim.

A cursed object is something the demon was given the right to attach to by the person with authority over that object. If one suspects that the right is based on the presence of a cursed object, the minor exorcism can be said over the object by a priest, it can be destroyed, or it can be removed from the premises to test whether it is the salient object in the case. In that test the manifestations should stop while it is off the property.

3) Demons will not stop interfering with a person or space until told to leave explicitly by the authority of God through the ministry of the Church.

Once an individual has made an agreement with evil spirits, legal rights belong to the demon until the rights have been removed. Only then can the demons be exorcised and cast away.

An appearance of leaving on their own is a deception designed to make people drop their guard or go away. Satan can gain rights to a physical space from serious repetitive sin committed there, explicit consecration to Satan in black magic, invitation to spirit communication with random spirits, or through bringing a cursed object into the space. When Satan has gained rights to a space, demons will stay in that space until those rights are removed.

PRETENDING TO BE THE DEAD

The most common con game demons play is pretending to be the souls of dead people. Usually they pretend to be a recently-deceased loved one the person desperately misses. Grieving can cause a person to think less rationally and drop their emotional guard. This con can be done directly, or through a third party, and usually includes specific information "only they would know."

If the con is through a third party, this is usually a "medium" or "psychic" who claims to be able to talk to the dead, or "channel" them. Usually these people are simply con artists who say things common to the human experience to a room of one hundred-plus people and cause amazement that someone present matches that scenario. This is called "cold reading" and can include things like,

"Someone here is close to a Jim . . . a John . . . a J name?" or "Someone here lost someone last month?" or "Someone had a difficult death and they are here for a Bob? Bill? A B name?" etc.

Being a "medium" usually means the person facilitates some communication directly with a spirit, through allowing it to write with their hand, talk with their mouth, or fully take over their body. This is usually faked or a self-induced trance, but can also be demons entering the person and providing information to draw more people into their web of deception.

In rare cases psychics have demons attached to them, usually from childhood, or that run in their family, that provide accurate and amazing information. In even rarer cases there are people who seem to have a gift from God and know information through a connection with God (think of many of the saints who knew things they could not humanly know). The two signs that a person is a con artist or working with demons is that they charge money and things only get worse as they get involved. If a person has a genuine gift from God they are almost never promoting themselves, charging money, or seeking attention.

If the con involves a direct interaction with the person, the demons may cause some manifestation around or with a person to make them think their loved one is there. This can include smelling an odor associated with that person, moving items that belonged to that person, giving a "sensed presence" experience, touching a person, speaking out loud in their voice, or even seeming to lay with them in bed.

One hallmark of a demon pretending to be a human spirit is that something will be hidden, missing, or deformed in the visual manifestation such as the head held down so hair hides the eyes, half the face slumped down, animal parts or aspects, or missing body parts.

OFFERING HIDDEN INFORMATION

Another powerful temptation is the offer of hidden information, especially when it involves the spiritual world and life after death. Many psychics play on this with cold reading and other techniques long since debunked by professional magicians. Some psychics have relationships with demonic spirits and so provide information that is often partially true and amazing to the receiver. There is no human power to know hidden things except through God or demons.

There have been many demonic cases that started after consulting psychics. By consulting a psychic, or doing divination themselves, one says to God, "I don't trust you; I am going to seek information, comfort, or power from another spirit." This is a rejection of God and the establishing of a relationship with a demon. Specifically, this is a violation of the First Commandment—"I am the LORD your God, . . . You shall have no other gods before me" (Ex 20:2–3).

Psychics draw the person into deeper and deeper dependence over time by warning of curses that are costly to remove or by stringing the person along for more information at future sessions. The psychic earns both more income and approval from the demons if they are knowingly working for them. It is important to understand that most psychics do not realize they are receiving their information from demons. Some even claim to be Catholics but apparently rationalize that they are special and different—and somehow exempt from God's rules in Scripture, particularly the First Commandment.

OFFERING COMPANIONSHIP

Demons may offer companionship, usually during youth or old age. Children who are neglected are sometimes approached by demons who take advantage of that emotional wound. They may first come as other children, but their eyes will often be hidden. They may even ask to use the child's body to feel sensations again, claiming they were once alive and children also. In older age, they may pose as a recently deceased loved one or spouse. The victim often drops their guard because they long to interact with their loved one again. This game is usually played until some interaction is engaged in, then the manifestations shift to fear-inducing and oppressive events.

In the case of long-possessed people, the demons offer the familiarity of a lifelong companion who tells the person what to do, shape how they feel, and is partially "them." Longtime demoniacs often say they don't know who they are without the demon, even though its presence was terrifying. This is probably why Jesus delivers people from demonic possession in stages, so they can adjust and stabilize at each stage of being more their real self.

OFFERING DISTORTED SEXUALITY

Demons seek ways to influence and control humans. One of the classic ways to do this is through a distortion of our God-given sexuality. For example, demons very likely have a large role in the pornography industry. They offer a distorted sexuality through pornography, but also in the cases of direct sexual interaction. The commonly known terms "incubus" and "succubus" come from the middle ages and the exorcists at that time. These are types of demonic attack, not types of demons. Sadly, this type of interaction is common in full possession cases and in many cases of black magic acts seeking such a spiritual experience. Though it is unsavory to mention such things, it is important to know that one must never give in to this interaction and go along with it. At every chance when the will can be exerted, one must resist and pray. It does not count if this happens in dreams because the will has not chosen and so there is no culpability (legal responsibility).

OFFERING POWER

A common con game played with the young, particularly the wounded and angry, is the offer of power. The satanic and demonic culture of black magic can resonate with internal feelings of neglect, hurt, and powerlessness experienced by many young people. What starts as a partially conscious expression of emotions can develop into a real relationship with the demonic.

Demons may offer strength, revenge, camaraderie, and approval to all the negative emotions someone is experiencing. The demons may pretend to be submissive and helpful, or under the control of the young black magician. But demons couldn't care less for symbols drawn on the floor, incantations, or gestures. None of this is binding on them and they mock witches and satanists during exorcisms as fools for falling for those tricks. Eventually a serious commitment is required, usually involving renouncing God, some personal sacrifice, and possibly vicious acts against purity and innocence. In some cases, allowing possession is required, usually facilitated by someone in a cult or coven, but it is sometimes done on the person's own accord. If the person allows possession, they are told they will then have the powers of the possessing demons at their whim: supernatural strength, knowledge of hidden things, skills, and influence over people. Of course, this ends up not being true.

PARANORMAL TELEVISION

We are currently living through a worldwide manifestation of the direct interaction con: the revival of the spiritualist movement. The first spiritualist movement in the western world was from 1848 until about 1900. This movement started with the Fox sisters, who had what seemed to be reproducible intelligent knocking in their home that responded to questions. It evolved into séances with mediums becoming a common pastime, as well as spirit boards and other games of spirit communication becoming commercialized. The spiritualist movement faded over time, partly due to the efforts of Houdini and others to debunk the fake mediums and their methods. There was a strong revival of interest after World War I (1914–1918) as the bereaved came to mediums seeking to speak with their lost loved ones. Then by the roaring Twenties the interest was all but gone.

On October 6, 2004, the first episode of the first paranormal television show aired. *Ghost Hunters* is a reality television show that follows a group of amateur "ghost hunters" on their investigations. Since its premiere, there have been dozens of shows that emulate *Ghost Hunters* all over the world.

The spiritual underpinning of each show varies, but usually the ideas that drive the content are vague and include experiences of "lost human souls," "intelligent hauntings" (a spirit you can interact with), "residual hauntings" (a kind of spiritual recording of past events you cannot interact with), and "demonic hauntings" (the TV version is usually anything that makes a growling noise on a recorder or results in a person being scratched).

Most shows stay away from demonic cases because they insinuate more of a religious perspective and advertisers do not like that. There is usually no religious approach to resolving the haunting that the people have called the paranormal group to help them with. Sometimes a resolution of the problem is attempted through telling the spirit to "go to the light" (which seems strange upon reflection . . . how does the command of the living, who have not seen the spiritual world yet, clear things up for that soul? If the dead could see "the light" and go toward it—if it were that easy— wouldn't they have gone there already?). The intentions of people are good, and they are usually just doing what they saw on television or the internet.

However, because of these shows, millions of people are developing distorted views about spirits and the methods used to supposedly record and interact with them. This model of understanding spirits is very naive and based on limited experience. The investigation methods used in the shows are centered on invitation to manifestation. They ask, command, beg, tease, mock, insult, or lure the spirit into revealing some sign of its presence. This sign can be a personal feeling or experience, but the goal is recording activity.

The most common evidence presented is electronic voice phenomenon (EVP). This is when an audio or video audio recording is made and later there are sounds that were not present when making the recording. In most cases the sounds are very faint, garbled, and hard to make out. This is typically because the noises are made by digital distortion accidentally caused by the "investigators" themselves or noise in the electronic circuit. Once it has been decided that something is being said—whether because anticipation is so great or because of the power of suggestion—the brain makes it seem more certain. In very rare cases there is a clear and distinct voice that is as loud as those actually present at the recording.

The second most common evidence presented is some unexplained noise that results in a dramatic, startled reaction by the people in the show. This is usually due to their being on edge in a dark place while listening intently for any sign of a spirit presence. There are numerous logical reasons for this alleged phenomenon, most of them having to do with noises that occur naturally when several people are walking around in old or abandoned buildings. It also doesn't hurt to create some human drama to make the show interesting enough to keep watching.

The third common type of evidence presented is visual: usually "orbs" or shadows. Orbs can be relatively easily explained. When cameras are in "night vision" mode they turn on an infrared light emitting diode to light the scene. This diode is designed to light a whole room; it is relatively bright (though humans cannot see infrared light). The camera automatically focuses on whatever is large and in its view; because of this, anything very close to the camera is out of focus. As a result of how these cameras operate, any dust or insect that goes by near the lens of the camera is blurry and lit very brightly compared to the rest of the scene, and so seems to be a glowing blob of light that moves. Orbs that show up on film and are sensationalized as ghosts or spirits on the show are almost always dust or bugs. The easiest way to confirm this is to stomp on the floor, wait ten seconds, and take another picture: voila, orbs.

Shadows are the other common type of visual evidence presented. Shadows can be tricky as the viewers of these shows aren't privy to all the behind-the-scenes work that is happening. Camera operators, crew members, and TV lighting are usually what cause these "unexplained" fleeting shadows, even if they are not causing them intentionally. Many of the television shows present false information, to say the least. People should be quick to dismiss their credibility and eagerly avoid them. These shows may seem like harmless programs, but in truth, no good can come from them.

SATANIC CULTS AND WITCHCRAFT COVENS

Beyond the individual con games demons play, there are deceptions facilitated by organized groups of people who are also deceived by demons. They generally fall into two groups: those who knowingly serve demons and those who have some level of misunderstanding and illusion about who or what they serve.

True satanists and witches are not people who read books on magic or wear gothic clothing—they tend to be in family-based groups that completely hide their activity and identity from the world.

In exorcism ministry we generally see three types of people from these groups:

- People in their late teens or twenties who have moved away from the cult or coven for school and realize there are other ways to live.
- Mothers who are having off-the-books pregnancies for the group and flee to protect their baby before it is born.

- Older people who are about to die and the demons turn on them after a lifetime of service because the person is no longer useful to them. These people usually ask to be separated from the demons before death because they now realize how the demons hate them and they do not wish to die connected to them.

The good news is that mercy is always there from Jesus, and time after time these people are freed. The desire to be free and choose God must be genuine, though—one cannot wallow in the demonic world their whole life and repent insincerely at the last hour. Repentance is ultimately between one and God.

✝

TYPES OF SPIRITUAL INTERVENTION

JUST AS THE DEMONS have many ways to attack us, we have a number of ways to defend ourselves. The most important of these ways is a proper understanding of the spiritual world, as this shapes intent and actions. People tend to have two basic approaches to the spiritual world: magical thinking and religious thinking. The essential difference is whether one's focus is on oneself or God.

Magical thinking assumes that if one knows enough information and then applies it through proper execution of behaviors and willpower they will achieve a result. Essentially, the thinking is "my will be done." There is usually no explicit need for God, but sometimes the power of God, usually in the form of angels or the name of God, are presumed to be recruited to serve the will of the person. These approaches vary quite a bit but essentially seek ways to force one's will onto the world through some form of personal power. Magical thinking often appeals to adolescents who feel powerless and have a need to individuate. One error that Christians sometimes make along these lines is to say that anything commanded to a demon in the name of Jesus must be obeyed, period. Experience shows that this is not the case with demons—if it were that easy, exorcisms and deliverance sessions would be over in one sentence. We cannot force our will on other people by commanding it, even in the name of Jesus, if they have not chosen to be free. God doesn't force us to not sin, or to reject a demonic problem; we must make those choices.

Religious thinking, on the other hand, assumes that God is the only authority and active agent and that people serve God's will. Essentially, "Thy will be done." In the religious approach one tries to be sure that any request fits God's rules and ways. One prays and asks God to do some action, then waits to see if God chooses to answer that prayer. The person is completely subservient to God in this approach as they understand that they are powerless on their own.

The language seen in exorcism seems to be from a magical-thinking perspective because it involves direct commands, but it is dependent on God's will. The exorcism is a sacramental and so does not have a guaranteed effect. Jesus—not the priest—exorcises the demon when He wishes. The exorcism is primarily dependent on the person choosing God and wishing to be free, and only secondarily on the command of the Church for the demon(s) to depart the person.

Many people who seek out an exorcist have a purely magical-thinking mindset, though they don't realize it. They assume that if they find the right priest with enough "power," their problem will be solved. They often assume that only an exorcism, and nothing less, will help them. This is placing human power or mechanistic ritual before their relationship with God. This may be part of why they have not received the assistance from God that they seek: God may be trying to correct their relationship with Him.

In resolving spiritual problems, it is imperative to first explore one's personal theology and correct any errors. A person's beliefs, assumptions, and attitudes are often key to the resolution. There are many ways that God might interact with a person and help them disentangle from a relationship with a demon. It is important to remember the big picture: God is completely aware of every individual situation and wants to help people to not only stop suffering, but to not repeat the errors that led to their problem. In cases of a demon attached to a family, we see that God wants to heal the family completely so that not only this person is freed but the next generation is as well.

People can be stuck at a certain point for some time. It is at those times they have to follow God's lead out of the situation. While there are many errors that lead to a continued or relapsed attachment to demonic forces, the most important thing to remember is that God is attempting to orchestrate disentanglement from both the demon and the misunderstandings that formed the relationship with the demon.

In every situation related to demonic problems, one should first establish a solid foundation of prayer, the sacramental life, the use of sacramentals, and blessings. Often this foundation, along with some theological formation and catechesis, resolves the case. People are commonly tempted to skip this foundation and the work it entails, and instead seek an exorcism to remove the problem. This usually leads the person back to the foundational problem, allows the demon to return, and only makes the problem worse in the long run.

RULES THAT WE SHOULD OPERATE UNDER

The legalism of the spiritual world becomes especially apparent when interacting with fallen angels. The Church has been doing this work for about two thousand years, building on the example and instructions of Jesus Christ, keeping track of experiences, centralizing the data, and codifying rules of engagement.

There are four main vehicles for the Church's wealth of knowledge in this area: Scripture, the instructions for the ritual of exorcism, the ritual itself, and verbal tradition. Most of the critical information lives in the verbal tradition and is passed on from teacher to student.

We can learn the most fundamental virtue for conquering evil through doing what Satan failed to do: obeying God. Always work within the Church's authority and instruction when opposing demons. By disobeying the rules, acting on personal authority, or using methods not approved by the Church, one flirts with disaster.

EXORCISM

Exorcism is a sacramental, defined in the Catechism under the heading "Various forms of sacramentals":

> When the Church asks publicly and authoritatively in the name of Jesus Christ that a person or object be protected against the power of the Evil One and withdrawn from his dominion, it is called exorcism. Jesus performed exorcisms and from him the Church has received the power and office of exorcizing. . . . The solemn exorcism, called "a major exorcism," can be performed only by a priest and

with the permission of the bishop. . . . Exorcism is directed at the expulsion of demons or to the liberation from demonic possession through the spiritual authority which Jesus entrusted to his Church. (1673)

Some rules about exorcists and exorcisms are provided by the Church in a few places. These show the caution and prudence with which the Church approaches and administers this ministry.

- Exorcisms may only be performed by priests who have specific permission from their bishop.[1]
- "A priest—one who is expressly and in special wise authorized by the Ordinary—when he intends to perform an exorcism over persons tormented by the devil, must be properly distinguished for his piety, prudence, and integrity of life."[2]
- Exorcists must study diligently and consult their own experience as well as the experiences of others before and during the process of deliverance and exorcism.
- No layperson is allowed to perform the official rite of exorcism or any part of it, even though it can now be found in the public domain.
- The lay faithful cannot dignify a demon by directly questioning it about its name or anything else.

---

[1] Canon 1172, Code of Canon Law at the Vatican website, accessed on 7/20/2017: http://www.vatican.va/archive/ENG1104/_P48.HTM.

[2] *Roman Ritual (Christian Burial and Office for the Dead, Exorcism, Blessings Reserved to Religious or to Certain Places, Volume 2)*, trans. Fr. Phillip T. Weller (Milwaukee, WI: The Bruce Publishing Company, 1952), 169; reprinted by Preserving Christian Publications, Inc., Boonville, New York.

Demonic influence *must* be revealed on its own, not searched for.

• Before beginning an exorcism, the signs of possession have to be distinguished from mental disturbance or medical illness. A licensed professional must evaluate people from their professional perspective and determine if a mundane diagnosis accounts for the symptoms. It is not the job of outside consultants to diagnose possession—that is the exorcist's job. In addition to ruling out medical and mental illness, some of the signs of possession must be documented. These are: the ability to understand or speak languages the person does not know, demonstrating knowledge of things the person could not know, and/or strength beyond the person's age and condition.[3]

• The victim of demonic influence or attachment should pray, engage in the sacraments, and express their choice for God.

Beyond priests and laypeople following these rules, God gives us powerful spiritual weapons to yield against the demonic.

PRAYER

Many, through no fault of their own, merely repeat the words of prayers in a mechanical way because they have never learned or experienced anything different. Prayer said against a demon that is not from the heart has little

---

[3] Introductory note 3 of the Weller translation of the 1952 Roman Ritual of Exorcism.

or no effect. A prayer said sincerely, in humility, with love and trust in God, is a scourge to the demon. The people involved in the case should be praying on a daily basis. Daily Mass, adopting the practice of praying the Liturgy of the Hours, and praying a daily Rosary for the situation is ideal. For priests, a Mass intention a week is a powerful help to the case. Monastic communities can also be a great boon to difficult or major cases. There is tremendous benefit in having a religious community praying for the case during confrontations with the demon. Sometimes religious are compelled by the Holy Spirit to pray for a case at just the right time without any knowledge of the schedule, and when they later ask what was going on during a particular day and hour, we realize that they had been praying during the time that exactly coincides with the exorcism. Fasting should be done, as advised in Scripture (Mk 9:29), but not to the extent that people are physically weakened or lose mental acuity.

As a general rule, people should seek the blessing of the priest as often as is reasonable. The home should be blessed yearly, as well as the mode of transportation. Blessed holy symbols should be in each room of the home. The faithful should wear blessed objects, but if a person is possessed this may not be possible. People should also seek indulgences when the Church makes them available.

SACRAMENTS

The sacraments, particularly the Eucharist and Confession, are very important for people struggling to disentangle from a demon and its effects. It is very common that people experiencing spiritual problems have drifted away from the sacraments. Confession can close many doors to the demonic and frees more people than exorcism by far. Forgiving the sins of others and letting go of anger can also be done in the context of a confession. It is common that, after confession and a prayer session, one spirit leaves and another is revealed. The next usually has different rights that the person now recalls, confesses, and so on. The disentangling from the Devil's frauds is very much like peeling an onion layer by layer.

In some cases a person is not baptized validly—or at all. The choice to become baptized should not be made out of fear or to resolve a demonic problem. Take great care to ensure that it is a valid choice for God. Baptism can be a powerful help in the process of a person being freed from demonic attacks.

The Eucharist is a potent sacrament for the afflicted and those assisting in their cases. Catholics involved in exorcism or deliverance ministry should be daily communicants, if possible. The Eucharist should be guarded against defilement in cases of possession and so is not brought near the demoniac during exorcisms.

Valid marriage can also provide the grace to persevere through difficult years in dealing with a possessed family member. Having an irregular marriage validated can be a source of grace and correction in the family life.

SACRAMENTALS

Unlike sacraments, the effect of sacramentals is not guaranteed. The faith and spiritual state of the people using them has an impact on their efficacy.

Sacramentals prepare us to better participate in the sacraments and receive graces from them. Sacramentals include blessings of people, meals, objects, and places.

Holy water and crucifixes are common sacramentals. The blessing accompanying another sacramental, the St. Benedict medal, asks that it be imbued with the property to drive away demons.

DISCERNMENT OF SPIRITS

Discernment of spirits is a gift of the Holy Spirit, that is, a charism. It can take many forms, such as the special awareness of the presence of spirits. It can also take the form of knowing information about spirits: their names, the number of spirits, the rights they have, and so on.

Caution must be taken because discernment of spirits can be partly or wholly imagination and so must be well vetted before it is relied on. The gifts of the Holy Spirit can become too closely associated with a person's sense of self-worth and purpose. Especially because of this, like other spiritual callings or gifts, discernment of spirits should be validated and tested. There have been cases where people with self-proclaimed gifts of discernment have caused great fear and confusion in people through false or misguided information.

Discernment is information that comes from God on a moment-by-moment basis for a ministerial purpose. God provides the information needed to complete some task that He has appointed one to do. If the information is not in support of a valid ministerial or presents itself as a constant flow of impressions, images, and words, then it is likely not discernment. There are rare people that seem to be able to provide valid information about almost any situation or person. Some of the saints seemed to have this gift, though often, such as was the case with Padre Pio, the revealing of private information frequently takes place within the context of Confession or at other times to help people spiritually.

The mechanism of discernment of spirits can take many forms. Some people need to touch the body of a person in order to detect information. Some look in the person's eyes and can see a spirit there. Some can know information from hearing the names involved in a case. Some receive information while in meditative prayer. Some have the gift of being able to physically see all kinds of spirits and so can simply report what the spirits are doing. These mechanisms for receiving information from God seem to be given and then developed over time into a full form. God gives these charisms at Baptism, they are activated in Confirmation, and then they may develop further over time.

One cannot make a gift of discernment come; it cannot be demanded from God or transferred at will from person to person. Authentic discernment of spirits should always be used at the service of God's will in a ministerial context.

✝

HUMAN SPIRIT HAUNTING

CATHOLICISM IS CLEAR on the existence of a soul that survives the body, an accounting before God, and an eternal condition in either heaven or hell. Catholics also believe in purgatory: a temporary condition for the soul that has passed personal judgment but still has the temporal component of sins to atone for before attaining the beatific vision. There is a tradition within the Church of offering Masses and prayers for the dead in order to speed this purgation.

Many of the saints wrote of apparitions of souls appearing to them asking for prayer, penance, or Masses in reparation for their sins. After these were completed the saint was often allowed a final visitation from these souls as they ascended to heaven. There are many Church-approved books describing instances of souls manifesting to the living to signal their need for prayer. *Purgatory* by Fr. F. X. Schouppe, S.J., is one example.

Though souls in purgatory have sometimes been allowed to speak to the saints, it usually does not happen to the average person. The Bible is clear about the prohibition against speaking to the dead (Deut 18:10–13). Doing so represents a loss of trust in God by seeking to bypass

Him and instead seek out the help of a lesser spirit or medium as a source of comfort, guidance, or information. This is a violation of the first of the Ten Commandments.

In the case of saints who have spoken to spirits, they did not summon spirits or seek guidance, information, or comfort from them. Once the spirit requested prayer, communication stopped on both sides. It is interesting to note that in most cases of spirit communication involving paranormal investigators, the first thing said by the spirit is: "Help me." Sadly, most people do not know how to pray for the dead and so no help is forthcoming. Any communication beyond this is almost certainly demonic deception.

Some other information about, and traits of, human spirit hauntings are:

- Souls in purgatory are non-destructive in their signals.
- Souls in purgatory do not make manifestations that are inherently terrifying; they usually limit them to a sound, a word, or a limited movement of objects.
- Souls in purgatory limit their interaction with humans to signaling a need for help, and in rare cases the need for a particular wrong to be righted.
- Souls in purgatory do not engage in prolonged communication or dialogue.
- Souls in purgatory do not attack people physically.
- Souls in purgatory do not attack religious or holy things.
- Souls in purgatory become completely still and silent when prayer or Masses are offered for them.

Some of the typical indications that a human soul in purgatory may be present are sounds of a person walking or pacing, odors that were associated with that person, knocks on the walls, and, in cases of suicide, a heavy and sad feeling in the area where the suicide occurred. There is almost always a lack of speech on the part of these souls outside of the single phrase "Help me" or "Yes" in response to the question "Do you need prayer?" The souls in purgatory are aware of God's prohibitions about seeking information from the dead (see Deut 18:9–14; Lev 19:31 and 20:6; Is 8:19; and others) and so would never draw the living into this sin by communication beyond a need for prayer or Masses.

The most common types of human spirit haunting cases are the souls of people who have committed suicide as well as murder victims. These souls usually create a very strong feeling and effect of sadness, depression, and malaise near where they died. They may cause some manifestation, such as knocking or banging at the time they died or when they are talked about. One has to be careful because demons can take advantage of a known suicide or murder and pose as the victim in that location. Also, a demon that helped encourage a murder or suicide could still be there. The other types of human spirit haunting that are common occur in churches and religious housing such as rectories or monasteries.

In many cases where people have engaged in paranormal investigations, signs both of souls in purgatory and demons are present. This is because the demons are attracted to places where people have attempted to communicate with spirits. By seeking occult knowledge from a spirit, people give demons license to manifest and respond. In these situations there is often an initial communication—

essentially, "help me"—followed by a pause and then some manipulative and deepening communication. In this situation a demon is simply taking advantage of an opened door. People will usually describe the initial non-destructive signals and their attempts to have dialogue with the spirit as being followed by an escalation of negativity and violence that led them to call the Church for help.

RESOLVING HUMAN SPIRIT HAUNTINGS

Cases that combine a soul in purgatory with predatory demons are complicated. These types of cases should be addressed by qualified clergy. In cases where the people are unwilling to stop their spirit communication, prayers for the dead or Masses can be offered but the demons will stay and facilitate the ongoing communication. The person's choice to continue spirit communication gives the demons the right to be present.

If a case seems to be a genuine human spirit haunting, the usual remedy is the Mass or praying the Office of the Dead in the location. It seems that it is often most effective to say the Mass in the place where the person died, but this is not required. An abbreviated subset of the Office of the Dead has also been used in many cases with success. These prayers need to be said in charity and love. Additional prayers may need to be offered as well.

†

DEMONIC INFESTATION

DEMONIC INFESTATION takes place when demons obtain the right to produce extraordinary manifestations in a specific location (their ordinary manifestation is temptation). It is important to rule out other situations before concluding the case is a demonic infestation. Some common situations that are mistaken for demonic infestation include poor wiring that causes strong electrical fields which lead to dizziness and nausea (usually in a basement where the wiring is in the ceiling), living or dead animals inside walls, broken equipment or vents creating unusual noises, and medical or mental illness. Some alleged cases are the result of self-induced hysteria from spending too much time watching horror and paranormal shows and movies.

As mentioned before, a demon's ordinary activity is temptation. However, once demons gain the right to be extraordinarily active in a place, they often pretend to be human spirits seeking communication. They sometimes mimic voices of people that live in the home or physically attack people. A demon will often pick one person to focus on. They may manifest only to that person to make others think the victim is imagining things. The intent of the

demon is to wear down and isolate their victim(s). Some
of the typical traits of demonic infestations are:

- **Black shadow forms of various sizes.** These can be
  the size of a mouse, a basketball, a child, an adult,
  or larger. They are usually solid forms that cannot
  be seen through. They sometimes float as a kind of
  rolling black smoke that does not dissipate, they
  sometimes seem to walk, and they can also glide
  along floors, walls, or ceilings. These are seen
  full-on and often by multiple people at the same
  time. Note that seeing shadows out of the corner
  of one's eye is usually just an artifact of the way
  the eye works, and not an indication of a demonic
  spirit.
- **Strange noises or voices.** People may hear their
  names called by members of the household who
  are not home. The hearing of voices talking to each
  other without being able to make out the words
  is also common. The demons can make growling
  or other strange, animal-like noises. Note that it is
  not uncommon for the brain to imagine voices in
  white noise such as a fan or vacuum.
- **Bad odors.** These odors are strong and very re-
  volting. The odor does not dissipate and does not
  linger where the demon was; it moves with it. It
  is important to rule out mundane possibilities and
  not conclude there is a demonic spirit just from a
  bad odor.
- **Demonic nightmares.** These are persistent, repetitive, and out of character for the person. They
  can usually be stopped by lightly applying holy
  water to the whole head before sleep. Note that it

is normal for many people to process anxiety and stress in life through bad dreams or nightmares. Having nightmares alone does not mean there is a demonic spirit in the home; this is a secondary sign seen along with more dramatic signs.

- **Physical attacks.** Sometimes people are choked or harmed more severely, causing wounds, bruises, or bleeding. These wounds are visibly different from fingernail scratches. Note that waking up with a bruise or scratch does not mean there is a demonic spirit in the home; many people can be bruised, scratched, or wounded by themselves or a partner during sleep.
- **Sleep deprivation.** Sleep deprivation is often caused by phenomena happening as the person is attempting to go to sleep. Demons will also interrupt sleep. Sleep deprivation is almost always present in demonic infestation or oppression cases.
- **Interpersonal tumult.** In cases of demonic infestation, people living on the site sometimes get into fights and arguments that come out of nowhere and stop when they leave the house, or when the case is resolved. Note that arguments or fights alone do not mean there is a demonic spirit present, especially if there is a history of such conflicts in the lives of the people living in the home.
- **Suicidal or homicidal ideation.** It is not uncommon for people to report compulsive thoughts or self-harm or harming others. This type of thinking stops when the people leave the house or room where the problem is. It is very important to talk with your family, doctor, or local police if one is feeling suicidal or homicidal. These thoughts alone

do not mean there is a demonic problem, and they must be addressed medically.

- **Attacks on holy symbols or items.** Often holy items will be damaged, thrown, or moved and sometimes disappear when there is a demonic infestation.

RESOLVING DEMONIC INFESTATION

Finding the cause of the case helps to undo the rights the demons have, but it is not always necessary. For instance, in some cases people move into a home and do not know what went on in the home previously that could have led to the problem. If there is an unknown ongoing problem, such as a housemate secretly engaging in black magic, it usually comes to light quickly once the blessings and prayers start. This is one reason that demonic infestations should be addressed by experienced and prepared people.

Some of the common causes of demonic infestations are:

- **Moving into a home where black magic was practiced.** In these cases, the home has been consecrated to the demons by the previous authority over the home. There may still (but not necessarily) be objects or words and images left behind; they are often hidden and can be difficult to find. These objects need to be exorcised and disposed of, or simply destroyed and disposed of. Destroy any black magic writing or images. Some homes were consigned to the Devil when they were constructed and have a history of destroying the lives of their occupants. This can also happen at businesses where the manager or owner practiced, or is practicing, black magic.

- **A curse being sent against an unprotected home or person.** A curse is simply a demon sent to do some harm. If the home is not blessed and there is little relationship with God, the demon may be able to have some effect there. If a demon is sent to harm a person who is in a state of grace, little or nothing happens. Anxiety about curses is common and should be avoided. Focusing on the demons gives honor to them and takes attention away from God. A healthy sacramental life combined with a prayer life in a blessed home is the best protection.

- **Bringing a cursed object home.** Cursed objects are objects that have had the opposite of a blessing done to them. Instead of grace being attached to an object to make it holy, a demon has been attached to the object to make it associated with evil. People sometimes unknowingly bring cursed objects home. Sometimes this is a gift or a new antique acquired around the time when the problems started. Generally, these objects can be exorcised by a priest and left in place. If the object is obviously evil in appearance it is probably best to destroy it also. It is good for the priest to then exorcise the home and do a thorough house blessing, including the blessing of the thresholds. Usually one can test if an object is causing the problem by temporarily removing it from the property.

- **Engaging in spirit communication in other locations, or in the home.** With the current paranormal craze it is not uncommon for people to do modern séances with electronic recorders or other devices. This spirit communication opens the door for random spirits to manifest and communicate. In some cases a demon accepts the invitation and starts the process of forming a relationship that leads to oppression and then possession, or suicide. Sometimes these people hear from souls in purgatory signaling for help in the beginning, but it is almost always demons that respond to their invitations. It is also common that one demon follows them and produces similar sounding "EVPs" everywhere they go. Those involved need to renounce spirit communication, get rid of all recordings, and ideally get rid of the equipment. Once these steps are done it is best to do a house exorcism, a house blessing, and the Epiphany blessing of the thresholds.

- **Being actively attacked by practitioners of black magic.** In rare cases a black magic coven actively attacks a family or person to drive them off a property or harm them. These cases should be well documented and handled in cooperation with law enforcement, as criminal activity is often involved.

- **Being afflicted by a relative.** In some cases a relative involved in black magic is causing the problem. The relative may have a conflict with the target of the infestation or oppression and is sending the demons to torment them. When this person is allowed to live in the home, it is difficult to resolve the case. This is because the person has been given the right to be present and so they have some authority to bring their spiritual problems with them.

- **Bringing a possessed person into the home as a guest.** In some cases families have taken in troubled people who needed help yet are possessed. This usually leads to signs of demonic infestation as the demons with that person have secondary rights to manifest where the person has been allowed to be. The person will often leave when the house and thresholds are blessed, as their demonic companions desire to depart.

- **An explicit invitation made for spirits to "come home with me" from another location.** This might happen during or after a "paranormal investigation" or other circumstances. The most common trick of demons in these cases is to pretend to be a little girl who lost her mother. This is because females are less threatening than males, and children are less threatening than adults, and it activates maternal instincts in women so that they often drop their guard.

- **Murder or suicide.** A murder or suicide can lead to a demonic infestation when the demon that inspired that action remains in the location. They generally do not remain if the house is blessed and the owner has a good sacramental relationship with God. Generally, a pattern will be seen where subsequent residents will have the compulsion to do a similar act, in the same way, even if they don't know the history of the house.

- **Other actions done by the person with authority over the land or building.** These can go far back in history in some cases. It is not necessary to discover all the details of the history since the current owner has authority now and can simply renounce everything that was done by previous owners.

Sometimes it is necessary for the priest to say the minor exorcism in a few locations in the building, but usually one is sufficient. The most troubled location is the best location to say the prayers. Usually everyone present will feel the evil pressure lift when the demons depart and a noticeable lightness and clarity in the air will be detected. In some cases, there is a pleasant scent of roses before, during, or after the exorcism (this is a positive encouragement from God and associated by most people with the Virgin Mary).

The process of helping people with demonic infestation usually involves some education and renunciation on their part before the case can be resolved. If the people opened the door to the demonic activity they need to learn the rules of the spiritual world and make a final choice to close that door. If people unknowingly move into a previously infested location, the exorcism of the place and blessings can usually be done right away.

It is not unusual for demonic infestations to persist or get worse after an initial visit. In about two-thirds of cases, multiple visits are needed. This is almost always due to the choices of the people with authority over the home. It can be helpful to start over and help them renounce additional layers of consent or relationship with the demons before doing more prayers or house exorcisms.

Some relapse scenarios are:

- **The spirits are invited back.** This might be done by someone with authority over the place due to a desire for the favors or manifestations of the spirits.
- **Someone in the home might still be aligned with the demons.** Their presence gives the demons permission to be present with them.

- There may be additional sins and activities that the people have not confessed and renounced.

†

DEMONIC OPPRESSION

DEMONIC OPPRESSION OCCURS when demons have gained and exercise rights to interact in an extraordinary way with a person. Demons often develop a relationship of consent with a person or family line over years before demonic oppression takes place. This is because the demons don't cause distress until they have gained enough rights to remain without the person's ongoing consent.

There are many causes of demonic oppression, including (but not limited to):

- **Ongoing spirit communication** with a supposed human spirit, spirit guide, totem animal, holy angel, or other deception tailored to a specific victim. The demon will initially provide tantalizing bits of information and be passive. Over time it will propose more ways to interact and start to be a little more assertive. It often will start testing the person by telling them minor things to do or not do. Eventually it will propose that the person allow it to speak to their mind directly, dropping whatever mechanism or tool is being used to communicate with it. Once this step is taken, it will increasingly mandate behavior and start to threaten punishment for disobedience.

- **Occult or black magic rituals.** When people engage in black magic in order to gain power from demons, the progression to oppression (and possibly eventually possession) is much faster than with spirit communication. The type of black magic does not affect the process; however, the most common types that lead to cases are ritualistic Satanism (not a philosophy, but worship of Satan), demonolatry (the worship of demons), and witchcraft (that may or may not acknowledge that the only spirits to appeal to outside of God are demons). Sometimes black magic is done to a person when they are a child or against their will. These cases are complex and should be dealt with by specialists and in cooperation with law enforcement if a cult or coven is involved.
- **Living in a location with a demonic infestation for a time and then forming a relationship with the spirits there.** Some people are fascinated by and welcome manifestations they discover in a house or apartment they move into. This leads to a progression of events similar to spirit communication.
- **Consecration of a family line to demons by a previous generation.** Sometimes an ancestor has promised their children or family to demons in exchange for something. It is not necessary to know who did this or what specifically they did. It is important to not become anxious about this idea, as a healthy sacramental life negates almost all negative spiritual effects from ancestors.
- **A life of deep and prolonged sin possibly com-**

bined with drugs or alcohol that weakens the mind of the person. Sometimes spiritual oppression can be seen after a life of hardened sin. Usually sin at this level causes incarceration and other negative consequences that overshadow the spiritual oppression the person also experiences.

- **The combination of being the victim of a curse while also being spiritually vulnerable (not being in a state of grace).** For example, an enemy convinces someone already leading an immoral life to ingest something that has a demon attached to it.

- **Submitting to non-Christian faith healers, psychics, "energy healers," mediums, card readers, or other occult practitioners.** When a person submits to people engaging in these practices, it is a violation of the First Commandment in a way: they are not trusting God and instead are submitting to a person with "special powers" or someone who claims to have a "spirit guide."

An example of how oppression may progress would be demons pretending to be human spirits and getting their victim to consent to them being allowed to do automatic writing with the victim's hand, and then later to speaking directly into the victim's mind. They may then offer assistance or psychic powers such as predicting the future (demons do not know the future but predict things they then arrange). The demon increasingly isolates the person from people that love them—and from God. They then start commanding their victims to not participate in prayer or religious activities. People close to the oppressed person may report abrupt and unusual fights and impulses to abandon them. Once the demon has secured enough rights, their communication shifts to commands and threats about most aspects of life. These threats are backed up with some form of pain, whether it be assault, torture, intrusive thoughts, or other punishments. The person's behavior is controlled more and more over time. The demons rarely offer anything positive at this stage.

As the oppression deepens the demons will almost always urge their victims to commit suicide. Suicide is likely the best chance to permanently separate a soul from God, but it is not guaranteed as the Church has recognized that the choice to commit suicide is usually not made when a person is in his or her right mind (see *CCC* 2282–2283). Killing humans is not a win for the Devil. The soul cannot be taken to hell by demons, even in cases of full possession leading to suicide. A soul is separated from the demon and judged on its own merits at the time of death. The soul belongs to God and only He determines what happens to it.

The demons may suggest that consenting to full possession will end the suffering of the oppressed person. The demons isolate, torture, and wear the person down to break them so they give in. The person may not be able to eat much, or at all, they will sleep little and poorly, and they may be violated in other ways. While this is going on, they hear constant, horrible diatribes against God, religion, and prayer in their minds from the demons.

RESOLVING DEMONIC OPPRESSION

People suffering from demonic oppression are generally in great distress. They have often lost the ability to work or to live with their loved ones. They often have secondary health and mental health problems. They may despair of help and feel that God has abandoned them. Getting them to trust God and really reach out in prayer can be difficult. Some oppression cases can drag on for years or decades, but usually these are the cases that come from deep forms of union with a demon as a result of black magic in some form.

The treatment of demonic oppression involves similar steps as those undertaken in infestation cases. The key difference is that the oppressed person is at least partially deluded by the demon's mental games. The victim needs to be educated on the rules of the spiritual world, trust Jesus, renounce their relationship with the demons, fully engage in the sacramental life, and pray. An out-of-order spiritual life is usually the root of the issue. Deliverance prayer is not a bad thing in these cases, but it is not usually effective until the person really trusts God and turns away from the demon and all its lies. In cases of consecration by an ancestor, renouncement on that person's behalf and deliverance prayer against oppression is appropriate.

Cases of demonic oppression can be difficult for priests and those who assist them to deal with as people are often demanding about what they think needs to be done. They may insist on the priest performing an exorcism as they have seen on television or in the movies, and many see exorcism as a form of magic. These people are sometimes resistant to being educated about the difference between oppression and possession and about when an exorcism is appropriate.

Since in demonic oppression there is often some form of hallucination present, as well as suicidal ideation, it is important that proper medical and psychiatric supervision be provided. There are many medical and psychological problems that are misunderstood as demonic oppression. The first step in any case is to have medical and psychiatric causes ruled out. Next, the details of the case are compared with what is known about demonic oppression. Confirming demonic oppression can be difficult as objective data is often not as discernible as it is in possession. These cases need to be examined by people with experience evaluating spiritual cases as well as some general experience with troubled people.

Once some certainty is established that the person is oppressed, those assisting need to focus on helping the victim of oppression uncover any lies the demons have led him or her to believe. These may include lies about the identity of the demon, the notion that the person's endless suffering is special and willed by God, or that there is no help for them in the Church. The deception is tailored to the particular person. They need to disentangle from these deceptions as they are designed to further the relationship with the demon. In addition to addressing the demonic lies, the oppressed person needs to fortify their spiritual life, first with confession, then the renewal of baptismal promises, regular participation in the Mass, and the development of a solid prayer life.

It is important for the person to repent of their sins and also forgive the sins of others. Demons hold on to both our sins and our unforgiveness of other people's sins.

Once the lies are undone, sins are repented of and forgiven, and the person renounces the relationship with the demon, the oppression usually lifts. The priest can also pray informally over them, asking Jesus to free the person from their affliction. There are no set deliverance prayers for this, but the combination of the sacramental life, the renunciations, and a general prayer to Jesus asking for the liberation of the person should be effective.

If the case of oppression is well progressed, the person

may have transitory states of demonic manifestation when they are prayed over, or turn out to be completely possessed. When this is true the demon may be agitated by prayer or sacramentals and show itself by speaking or vocalizing. It is typical for the person to show other signs of oppression at this time as well.

Once a person is showing possible signs of demonic manifestation in their body, the case should be turned over to the diocesan exorcist for evaluation. When a priest is praying for an oppressed person and there is any indication that the victim may actually be possessed, that priest may not use the minor exorcism (or Leonine exorcism) over the person.

†

DEMONIC POSSESSION

WHEN A PERSON makes an informed, free choice to give demons the rights to control a body that person has authority over, the resulting state is called demonic possession. Demonic possession is qualitatively different from demonic oppression. Usually the choice that grants possession relates to the person's own body, but a parent or ancestor can also promise a family line or a child to the enemy. The demons can be present in a body but not have the rights to take it over; they need explicit permission for that. Once rights are given, demons can take over the body and use it at will, causing hallucinations, creating false memories, inserting thoughts, and generally affecting the body. The victim's free will is never extinguished, but the expression of their free will may be attenuated. For instance, a person can always ask for help, but they may be limited to signaling so instead of speaking it.

A demon that has a body to use is much more dangerous than a disembodied demon. Exorcisms are always dangerous, and it is possible that God will allow harm in rare cases. At the beginning of the solemn exorcism the demon is commanded that they may not harm the priest, the assistants, their loved ones, or anyone's belongings.

Full possession usually emerges out of explicit satanism or witchcraft of some kind, often in family-based cults or covens. The possessed person usually has been victimized, has personally done terrible things, and in their possessed condition lives a nightmare of distorted perceptions, torture, and blasphemy. In addition, they often have false memories of experiences or images created by the demons to deepen their self-hatred and suicidal thoughts, as well as hatred for the things of God—particularly the priesthood and the Church.

The classic signs of possession are supernatural strength, knowledge of all languages, and knowledge of hidden things. Detection of holy objects and symbols is also very common. In practice, the demon has to be driven forward in order for the first three signs to be seen. Usually tests for detecting the holy (without the person knowing something holy is near) is the only test that can be done outside of an exorcism or minor exorcism.

One additional rare sign can be mentioned here: levitation. The most common form seems to be when the body rises off the floor and floats six to ten inches off the ground, gliding across the room and moving like a snake. Another form is floating straight up into the air, usually many feet up. Variations of this are when a person moves up a wall, sticks to the wall, or walks on walls or ceilings. A number of saints could levitate; it is not an inherently evil phenomenon. Like most preternatural manifestations this is a counterfeit or mockery of something holy.

Some aspects of exorcisms are important to understand when considering the dangers and complexities of the situation. During exorcisms there are many psychological games, tricks, and manipulations that the demons use. They very often lie or partially lie to anyone except the priest who carries the bishop's authority to perform exorcisms. When the priest who carries the Apostolic authority commands a demon to answer a question relevant to the case, the demon either gives the right answer or remains silent; they can almost never lie in those instances. If they remain silent it is almost always because some right or bond between them and the person is still in place. If the priest asks a question out of curiosity that is not related to helping that person be liberated, the demon may lie because the priest has stepped outside of what the Church prescribes.

The free will of the demoniac is central to the success of the exorcism. God does not violate free will and so one must be fully committed to choosing God and rejecting the demon. The victim should pray, engage in the sacraments (as much as they are able), and express their choice for God. One tactic of the devil is to punish the person for the exorcisms. The demoniac needs to bear up under any punishment the devil is allowed to exact on them, always focusing on Jesus. One danger here is that the devil may encourage the person to continue the possession because their suffering is "special" and willed by Jesus to make them a "victim soul." They may think that Jesus wants them to retain the possession and the pains that go with it. This is a demonic lie designed to trick the person into remaining possessed.[4]

---

[4] Roman Ritual, General Rules Concerning Exorcism, Rule 12: "The subject, if in good mental and physical health, should be exhorted to implore God's help, to fast, and to fortify himself by frequent reception of penance and Holy Communion, at the discretion of the priest. And in the course of the exorcism he should be fully recollected, with his intention fixed on God, Whom he should entreat with firm faith and in all humility. And if he is all the more grievously tormented, he ought to bear this patiently, never doubting the divine assistance."

The aftercare for a person is as important as the pastoral process during the case. Those involved should pray for spiritual healing of the person immediately after exorcism and the person should devote energy to their spiritual life and its improvement over time. They should participate in the sacraments and guard themselves with frequent prayer. The first weeks after freedom are often the most critical as the demons will try to make some bargain or offer to gain permission to re-enter the person. The person or team responsible for aftercare needs to discuss this with the former demoniac and help them stay strong against any attempts by hell to renew the possession.[5]

POSSESSION CASE TYPES AND RESOLUTION

Possession cases can be complicated and they can change over time. That being said, there are some common antecedents to possession:

- An indwelling of demons in the body from birth due to consecration by ancestors or parents. If followed by free will choices, the indwelling demon is free to possess the body; usually these choices are to engage in the sins that demons specialize in.
- Participation in black magic, especially involving the worship of demons or Satan. These cases arise from people explicitly inviting possession, usually in exchange for some favor from the demons, such

---

[5] Roman Ritual, General Rules Concerning Exorcism, Rule 21: "Finally, after the possessed one has been freed, let him be admonished to guard himself carefully against falling into sin, so as to afford no opportunity to the evil spirit of returning, lest the last state of that man become worse than the former."

as power. The possessed person will often come to the Church for help later in life when the demons turn on them because the victim is no longer of use.

- Deep occult involvement. Usually occult involvement alone only leads to oppression but it can evolve into possession over time. When a demon is already present in the family line, these sins compound the problem and can quickly lead to possession.

- Satanic ritual abuse usually arising out of family-based satanic cults or family-based witchcraft covens. Cults and covens raise children in an environment of systematic torture, psychological conditioning, and black magic. These cases usually involve younger adults who seek help when they first spend time in the world on their own and start to rebel against the path they were forced onto by their families in childhood. These cases can be very dramatic and may require working with law enforcement. Consulting with experts in this area is highly advised as some of these cases are actually traps orchestrated by the demons and the person pretending to seek assistance, designed to destroy those who seek to provide help.

- In cases where a person is very spiritually vulnerable (not baptized, steeped in mortal sin, and perhaps dabbling in the occult), a curse may lead to severe oppression and possibly possession over time.

In the history of the Church we see from the lives of some saints that God allowed possession as a *brief* trial in the advanced spiritual life. While this is very rare, it is important to remember that all demonic activity can be turned against the devil and used by Jesus for spiritual benefit and the ultimate glorification of God. Jesus never encountered a possessed person in the Gospels and left them possessed. He always freed them.

Possession is a complicated phenomenon and most cases involve many different spiritual legal rights and complicating factors. Jesus is aware of everything; He provides protection, intervention, and information to resolve each case.

Once a person is possessed, usually there is a significant change in them that is noticed immediately by the people around them. If they were possessed since childhood it may be harder to detect outside of prayerful situations. The demon-possessed person may attack family members, terrorize people, mutilate themselves, attempt suicide, disappear only to return in a daze, write bizarre things on the walls, speak foreign languages, and myriad other things. The demon can pretend to be the human they are possessing, perfectly mimicking them for a time.

Generally, a possessed person is incapable of asking for help from the Church and it is family, doctors, or friends that ask on their behalf. [6] If a person talks with a priest and asks for an exorcism, it is likely that they don't need one. A possessed person usually cannot talk with a priest, let alone discuss these issues, without being choked or having other manifestations stop the communication before it

---

[6] Roman Ritual, General Rules Concerning Exorcism, Rule 7: "At times, moreover, the evil spirits place whatever obstacles they can in the way, so that the patient may not submit to exorcism, or they try to convince him that his affliction is a natural one. Meanwhile, during the exorcism they cause him to fall asleep, and dangle some illusion before him, while they seclude themselves, so that the afflicted one appears to be freed."

even starts. The exception to this is people who have been possessed a long time and struggle to live a devout life. These people can often talk with a priest and ask for help, though internally they feel resistance to doing so. The central component of the pastoral treatment of possession is the solemn exorcism ritual. It is not often a one-time event, but rather a recurring cycle of education, renouncement, exorcism, and aftercare. Prayer, fasting, and penance should also be offered for the support of the case. Through the grace of God and this prayer support, the person is often allowed to have some limited conversations with the priest and even to make a confession. As much of the sacramental life as possible should be engaged in.

While this process is ongoing, the demons are also active on the other side of the case. They have twenty-four hour access to the mind and body of the demoniac and constantly assault their victim with illusions, lies, and partial information to convince them to stop working with, and to distrust, the Church. While the demons are manipulating the demoniac, they are also trying to manipulate the priest, usually by leading him down roads of inquiry about legal rights that are fruitless, or inciting curiosity about novel methods or theology in the exorcism ministry.

The best weapons in the pastoral process of exorcism are *humility, obedience,* and *prayer.* One needs to stay humble and remember that Jesus Christ is the exorcist. The priest must stay obedient to the Church and simply follow the exorcism ritual as it is given. During the pastoral process outside of the exorcism, prayer must be sincere and frequent. Every case is different and the Holy Spirit needs to help the demoniac expose each layer of deception and sin that needs to be addressed. Because cases are resolved over time, the person is able to heal and adjust to becoming gradually disentangled from both the demons and their manipulations.

Exorcisms usually go on for six months to two years of weekly sessions, and severe cases can go on for a decade or more if the person cannot renounce all the ties to the demons. Exorcism is a long process of unraveling the various lies and manipulations that the demons have instilled in their victims. It involves casting out many demons over time. Eventually the demonic "manager" of the case is confronted, and in rare cases Satan comes to fight for the case after all other demons are expelled.

EXORCISM AND DELIVERANCE MINISTRY

Deliverance and exorcism are two different forms of spiritual intervention. Deliverance is a broad term that can mean being freed from any problem of a spiritual nature or cause. Here it will be defined as deprecatory prayer (a request) offered with the hope that God will free a person from a spiritual affliction.

Over the last fifty years or so, most deliverance work was done by Protestant denominations, and the books on deliverance over that time were from those perspectives. One erroneous idea that comes out of this tradition is that anything commanded to a demon by a baptized Christian in the name of Jesus will be obeyed immediately. This is a magical-thinking approach as it doesn't take into account the free will of the person in relationship with that demon. We cannot foist our choices onto other adults; they have their own free will. In some Protestant books on deliverance, one is encouraged to speak directly to, and command, the demons. This is imprecatory prayer, a direct command. It is critical to understand that imprecatory prayer directly commands a demon, which is a tacit acceptance to a personal battle with that demon, while deprecatory prayer asks God to act against the demon. The Catholic Church has understood that the full authority to command demons was given to the Twelve Apostles, therefore a priest needs Apostolic authority given to him by a bishop before he engages in a battle with a demon. Of course a bishop, cardinal, or pope can do an exorcism at any time.

It is easy to become distracted by the drama of deliverance and exorcism and lose sight of the fact that the source of demonic problems is a relationship with sin, and usually involves the First Commandment. It is often the case that, over time, emotional wounds lead to sin, which becomes habitual. The person grows in the wrong direction, like a tree that is bound and canted to the side as a sapling. The deception of the demon is to hide in these wounded feelings and distorted sense of self, seeming integral and necessary while fomenting more harm. People affected by demons must begin their healing by letting go of their own sins through repentance and of the sins of others through forgiveness.

The cycle of repentance and forgiveness is bolstered by reaffirming one's loyalty to God, such as with the recitation of the Apostles' Creed, the renewal of baptismal promises, and participation in the sacraments. God works with the person where they are and they are usually given as much insight into their own wounds and sinfulness as they can handle at the time. It is like training that tree to now grow in a new way: change too fast and the tree breaks.

A common challenge in deliverance and exorcism ministry is discerning whether a case is possession or severe oppression. Just below full possession, a person may manifest to some degree contorting, growling, reacting somewhat negatively to sacramentals, and hints of other indications of possession. However, in cases of full possession we see the demon taking over the body completely: supernatural strength, occult knowledge, knowledge of all languages, and detecting the holy.

It is important to understand the difference between an exorcism and a *solemn* exorcism. An exorcism is an imprecatory prayer (a command), such as the exorcism in the Sacrament of Baptism. A solemn exorcism is a liturgical imprecatory ritual provided by the Church for treating demonically possessed people. Trouble arises when well-intentioned people presume to be able to perform something resembling a solemn exorcism to aid in cases of demonic oppression or possession. Liturgical prayer is reserved to clergy, and the Church limits imprecatory prayers against demons to priests with authority from their bishops.

In 1890 Pope Leo XIII added the "Exorcism Against Satan and the Fallen Angels" as an appendix to the solemn exorcism. The Leonine (or "minor") exorcism is effective in resolving demonic infestation cases. It has also been used, with permission from the ordinary, as a diagnostic test of possession in cases that are not yet clear. Not just any manifestation in response to the Leonine exorcism is sufficient evidence of possession; one or more of the traditional signs must still be documented. At no time should the public use this prayer as a way to test for possession; it must only be used by a priest with permission from his bishop. There have been cases of lay people becoming possessed as a result of using the minor exorcism over a possessed person.

The Church provides deliverance from oppression cases, even just under full possession, primarily through reception of the sacraments and spiritual direction. The affected person contributes greatly to their liberation through fully embracing spiritual guidance, confession, forgiveness, prayer, penance, and the Mass. When a person starts to exhibit demonic manifestations, the case should be referred to the bishop's office. Even though the case may not rise to the level of full possession, the bishop's office or appointed personnel can oversee the spiritual direction and monitoring of the case.

In the instructions to the priest in the Roman Ritual, the priest is warned to not too readily believe that a person is possessed and to consider whether they are suffering from mental illness. The Church requires that an investigation be made to ensure that the symptoms cannot be explained by mental or medical illness and that at least some of the four signs of possession are also present.

THREE SIGNS OF POSSESSION

The Roman Ritual cites only three signs:

1. Ability to speak with some facility in a strange tongue or to understand it when spoken by another. Fallen angels are immortal spirits and have existed since the beginning of creation. They either have the faculty of all languages from observing and interacting with people throughout history or through some other mechanism. It is important to differentiate between knowing a bit of a language and having facility with it beyond what is reasonable. In one case, a demon inside a high school-educated rural adult in the United States correctly responded to questions in English, French, Latin, Lithuanian, and German. Sometimes the demons will use languages that the priest does not know to answer questions. In this way they both answer the question and don't. The simple solution to this is for the priest to command them to answer in his native language.

Demons are also wont to correct people's use of languages when they make mistakes, taking pleasure in mocking them. For instance, they may mock translators when they miss the nuance of a translation or they might correct a person's Latin.

One additional language phenomenon sometimes happens in response to praying in tongues. The demon may start speaking back in its own form of "prayer," a demonic version of tongues. While praying in tongues usually consists of a few syllables or phrases that are repeated, the demonic version sounds more like a complete language. It is very disturbing to hear and hard to describe; it is a kind of hissing, lilting language.

2. The faculty of divulging future and hidden events. The most common form of divulging future and hidden events is when demons recount events for which the demoniac was not present. Sometimes they reference what the exorcist was doing in between sessions. They may reference other cases or what a different demon said or did in a different exorcism case. The sins of the victim are usually cited by the demon as the basis for its legal right to continue to stay with that person; however, they *usually* do not recite the unconfessed sins of the priest or assistants. Confessed sins are either hidden from the knowledge of the demons or not legally allowed in argument. One good side effect of revealing the sins of the victim—whose mortal sins in particular leave them vulnerable—is that they can now be worked on in confession, through penance and forgiveness.

No one but the exorcist should speak to the demons if

they address people about their sins—during an exorcism or at any other time. The demons are simply trying to goad people into interacting with them.

The demons sometimes seem to divulge future events, but they do not know the future. Although they may predict some event (almost always something negative), it is simply because the demon knows that their "prediction" will prompt the event to happen at the appointed time, or they go and cause the predicted event. In other cases, they predict things that are determined before they happen, such as the next song on the radio.

3. Display of powers which are beyond the subject's age and natural condition. This sign is usually interpreted as preternatural strength. There is a danger of slipping into a fearful mindset when considering this aspect of possession. The demons are always restricted by God and can only do as much as God allows. Sometimes God allows the demons to struggle powerfully with those assisting the priest; it might take four or five large men to restrain a person. In other cases the possessed person may obey the command to sit with their hands in their lap and require no restraint. The important thing is to stay focused on God, not the demons.

A fourth sign commonly used, but is not specifically cited in the ritual, is the detection of the holy. Examples of this include knowing that some concealed object is blessed, identifying the saint whose relic is in the room, identifying the sacramentals carried secretly by the priest (a St. Benedict medal, for instance), reacting to prayers said only in the mind, and so on.

†

SELF-HELP

IT IS COMMON for people to believe they are having an extraordinary spiritual problem when the issue really is an undiagnosed (or untreated) medical or mental health problem. But even where genuine extraordinary spiritual problems exist, mental health problems can also be present. Therefore it is very important that one remain open-minded about the possibility of medical or mental health issues and cooperate with treatment.

Spiritual self-help can be organized into four general categories: preventative measures, corrective measures, avoiding false religions, and avoiding violations of the First Commandment.

PREVENTATIVE MEASURES

Preventative measures are based in broad attitudes and actions that comprise the regular, balanced Catholic life. They include:

- Participating in the sacramental life. For laypeople this means Baptism, Confirmation, and Reconciliation, as well as the Eucharist on Sundays and holy days of obligation.

- Remaining in a state of grace. This means avoiding mortal sin and repenting of mortal sin when we do not avoid it. Mortal sin (the knowing and willful violation of God's law in a serious matter) causes spiritual death and a separation from God. We restore our spiritual life by repenting in the Sacrament of Reconciliation. The state of grace is removed when we have unconfessed mortal sin on our soul. Venial sins are slight sins which do not break our friendship with God the way mortal sins do, although they harm it.

- Maintaining a balanced and healthy prayer life— with the help of the Divine Office, the Rosary, or other daily prayers—is an important preventative measure. A healthy prayer life is comprised of prayers of praise, petition for ourselves, intercession for others, and thanksgiving to God. The prayer life should arise from a desire to pray in these ways, not from a fear of demons or a sense of desperation.

- Developing a proper understanding of the spiritual world and becoming educated in spiritual and religious matters (catechesis). This is helpful for people suffering from extraordinary demonic problems because it removes the fear-based idea that demons are free to do as they wish. Catechesis empowers us with knowledge and a sense of what actions to take.

- Making use of sacramentals and blessings. Homes should be blessed thoroughly. Thresholds should be blessed each year at Epiphany. Holy water and blessed salt should be in the home and used as needed. A blessed holy symbol, perhaps a crucifix, should be prominent in every room. A consecration of the home to the Sacred Heart of Jesus and the Immaculate Heart of Mary can be done, but this ceremony also calls for a commitment from the family to live in a certain way, so it should only be done if all of the family members are in agreement.

CORRECTIVE MEASURES

The primary corrective tool for people is Confession followed by Mass. Usually everything up to possession can be resolved through a healthy sacramental life and regular prayer. Moving a person out of the state of grace is the goal of temptation, and confession can move them back into the state of grace, preparing them to fully participate in the Mass where the greatest graces are provided.

Some oppression cases also require deliverance prayer. Deliverance prayer should be used after the foundation of the sacramental life is established. Deliverance prayers are essentially a request to Jesus to help a person with a problem. Experience has shown that it is best to leave the laying on of hands with prayer to a priest. Problems with the demonic have occurred from laypeople laying hands on a possessed person and praying against the demon. Consecrated hands and the backing of the bishop's apostolic authority is needed to do this safely.

For cases where the poor souls may be manifesting a need for prayer, the primary assistance for them is the Mass. Saying the Office of the Dead, by clergy or laity, can also resolve human spirit hauntings.

For demonic infestation, the sacramental life is usually not sufficient as the infestation affects the home and not the person living in the home. House exorcisms are approved when demonic infestations are verified, though there are no fixed rules or signs required. Only a priest can do the minor exorcism of places (the Leonine exorcism). There are some websites and phone apps that falsely tell the public that they can say the Leonine exorcism. The use of the minor exorcism was restricted by then-Cardinal Ratzinger (later Pope Benedict XVI) in 1985.[7]

If there are any cursed objects, removing, exorcising, and/or destroying them is usually necessary. If an object is valuable or cannot be removed it should at least be exorcised. The only corrective measure for possessed people is the solemn exorcism, as stated. It is worth reiterating that the solemn exorcism for a person can only be said by a priest with permission from his bishop. It is gravely dangerous to attempt to perform a solemn exorcism outside of these conditions.

AVOIDING FALSE RELIGIONS

There are several false religions or spiritualities in the world. It's important to guard against falling into them, as they are almost always pathways to demonic interaction.

Every measure must be taken to guard against the false promises of Satan in black magic, which has become readily available online and promoted in the media. Avoid the offers of power, information, control over demons, and

---

[7] Saying the Office of the Dead or offering Masses for the repose of souls in purgatory that are signaling the living resolves human spirit hauntings quickly and easily.

worldly success. These supposed benefits of demonic relationships may be provided in the short run, but are followed by crashing further down than where you started. The demons feign obedience and lie in order to draw people into worshipping them, use their victims, and then turn on them.

Guard against media that is actually veiled demonolatry (the worship of demons) or black magic. This includes things like occult films, depictions of magic rituals, books that glorify magic and demons, or occult music events. There is a disturbing trend of increasingly explicit black magic indoctrination at music festivals in Europe and the United States.

There are many cults that mix Catholic saints or devotions with pagan systems or explicitly demonic entities. They often use some Catholic symbols, or altered Catholic symbols, to insult God and to gain some amount of acceptability and legitimacy. One of the best known is Santa Meurte, a very large religion that sprung up in Mexico. Followers worship a skeletal female figure that is reminiscent of the Virgin Mary. Though there are many false religions and cults, the games of the demons are the same. The deceptions of the Devil are usually based on pride: for instance being "chosen" in a cult to play a certain role or being identified by spirits as a powerful magician that can control them.

Many New Age and pagan practices that are advertised as healing or healthy are spiritually dangerous. For example, Kundalini Yoga teaches that a serpent spirit is at the base of the spine and after activation from the touch of a yogi master rises to the head. This then causes uncontrolled movements and vocalizations. Similarly, Reiki healing has led to a number of possession cases, often after years of well-meaning work. Other occult powers beyond healing are involved in the higher levels of Reiki that are usually not taught to Westerners.

AVOIDING VIOLATIONS OF THE FIRST COMMANDMENT

Divination (fortune telling) and necromancy (supposed communication with the dead) are the two most common traps that people fall into that violate the First Commandment. This is because they both address people's primary fears of death: fear about their own future or sadness at the loss of a loved one. Going to psychics or having mediums speak to dead loved ones can open doors to demonic problems. Trying to communicate with the dead opens the door to a relationship with demonic spirits since any poor soul in purgatory would not draw a person into violating the First Commandment.

People that use divination based on using their own body as instruments of their practice usually develop problems faster. Examples include talking boards, pendulums, trance mediumship, lean testing, grip testing, and other similar activities. These are particularly dangerous because they give spirits permission to move part of the body and those rights of control remain until properly renounced.

Paranormal investigating is essentially necromancy because it is an attempt to make the dead manifest and communicate. This opens doors to relationships with demons on a large scale; about 25 percent of all demonic cases come from paranormal investigating. Many of the participants on paranormal television shows have had demonic problems themselves but this is not revealed as part of the shows.

†

TURNING THE PAGE TO JESUS

THERE ARE MANY personal journeys to God, but they all pass through Jesus. The Christian life starts with Baptism—being made into an adopted child of God—then develops over the course of a person's life into the ministry appointed by God for that person. The gifts to perform that ministry are given at Baptism and further activated at Confirmation. The depth of a person's spirituality and how close their relationship to God grows is dependent on God's grace and that person's cooperation with that grace.

We see three main places where this Christian spiritual life is mapped out: the Bible, the Church Fathers (St. Anthony of the Desert, Evagrius Ponticus, and others), and the Carmelite saints (St. John of the Cross, St. Teresa of Ávila, and St. Thérèse of Lisieux). Usually, people first wrestle with the "sins of the flesh," meaning the basic drives of the body to pleasure. Then they wrestle with the mind, with the memories and the imaginations that arise from the passions of the body. Once the passions are extinguished the person goes into the desert (figuratively or sometimes literally) to face the devil personally, no longer through veils.

It is usually not a problem to meet the needs of the body; the problems come when we are enslaved by our needs and go from urge to urge without applying reason. When we do this, we are more like an animal than a human being. The first stage of the Christian spiritual life is to wrestle with the tendency to thoughtlessly pursue every urge without considering the consequences to us or others. We must first make this process conscious so we can consider it. This is why we fast. By fasting in some reasonable way, we force that urge into view and we see to what extent we are unconsciously letting it control us. The point is not to suffer, but to teach us that we are not brute animals helpless to selfishly respond to every urge of the body. This cannot be learned intellectually; it must be learned though the experience of mindfully waking up to what we are actually doing and why.

This process of wrestling with the yoke that might otherwise dominate our lives helps us in a number of ways. We realize that we will not die if we don't obey the body immediately in all things—that we are not babies anymore. By forcing the choice to act into reason by denying it, we gain the time to reflect on the consequences. We can look at the consequences for ourselves, for our future, and for others. The other thing that happens with most urges is that they weaken in a short time if denied, and as they fade our minds becomes stronger and the urges become weaker. Of course, physical appetite is just one place to practice this; the general insights and spiritual strength is then applied to more subtle drives. This process of exercising the will and driving our choices into the light of reason then reveals the next level: where the urge is coming from.

It is good and necessary to eat. It is when an urge becomes corrupted or blown out of proportion that it is a problem. Most of us eat far more than we need to. Why is that? The urge to eat has become corrupted by advertising, or by a certain experience, or by dealing with emotional pain by eating. Over time the natural urge may get larger and larger, and more deformed. The extremes of this are the eating disorders and obesity.

There are four places an urge can come from: its natural source (eat to live), memory (recalling a great food and now wanting to have it again), imagination (thinking of some new food experience), and demons. Something goes from a natural need to a passion or obsession when we allow our memory or imagination to become dominated by it. By either focusing on a particular fantasy or constantly being reminded of related fantasies, we can allow a passion to dominate us more and more. We can see this in many areas: eating problems, excessive drinking, use of pornography, sex addiction, gambling, and others. The key sign is that the passion is dominating the person without any effective rational thought or choice involved; they feel enslaved by their desires and cannot seem to make healthy choices related to them.

In order for morality to develop, the person must first learn that they are a rational being that can make choices about their actions. By stopping the cycle of blindly obeying every urge, the person not only becomes aware of themselves, but they also buy time in the midst of the urge to see where it is coming from.

This is the second stage of the spiritual life: identifying and removing the underlying disordered passions that drive bad behavior. Most disordered passions are natural urges that have been corrupted or inflamed beyond their usual nature. Wrestling with passions leads to insights about them—intellectual consideration usually does not.

Jesus alludes to this when he points out that we must go deeper than the prohibitions of the Ten Commandments: it is not just resisting a sin but quenching the desire to sin that is important (Mt 5:28: "But I tell you that anyone who looks at a woman lustfully has already committed adultery with her in his heart").

Once the passions are identified and made conscious, they tend to lose most of their power. By making ourselves aware of disordered passions, we bring them into the light and are empowered to make choices about them. We will never be completely free of urges, but they are often greatly diminished and so much easier to address and control.

Demons are responsible for exciting the memory and the imagination, and so enflaming them to be disordered passions. This is called temptation: a prompting to do something against God's law. Since God's law can be seen in its simplest form as "Love God and love your neighbor as yourself" (see Mt 22:37–39, Mk 12:30–31, Lk 10:27), it is easy to see how selfish urges go against God's intention for us. Following an inflamed urge toward pleasure is all about loving the selfish pleasure, not God or other people.

In the ancient Church, some Christians were able to make this spiritual journey while living in the world, but many physically left the developed world. We can see a number of examples of this in the Bible and the early Church; the most dramatic is of course Jesus himself, who went into the desert to fast for forty days and then be tempted by Satan face to face. We can also expect to be confronted by demons if we progress past quenching the disordered passions in our hearts. In a sense, we cut off the entryways into ourselves that the demons use (the senses and the imagination), and they are forced to appear openly outside of ourselves and speak plainly. We are never completely free of inroads for temptation though—even ascetic monks have to combat their memories.

Jesus gives us instruction through His example: use the Word of God to counter each temptation. Evagrius Ponticus (AD 345–399) was an early Desert Father who wrote *Talking Back: A Monastic Handbook for Combating Demons*. This book lays out specific Scriptures to counter many dozens of the common temptations a desert monk may experience, as well as the physical manifestations of demons.

So we now see there are at least two ways to experience the extraordinary action of fallen angels: by entering into relationships with them or by closing off their access to tempt us so they are forced to confront us face to face. We usually choose to enter into relationship with them because we are uneducated about the spiritual world and because we have left our passions unchecked and allowed sin to drive us like a slave master. Many of us tend to be unaware of how God chooses to give us grace and peace, and many ignore the sacraments and the difficult journey of the spiritual life. It seems most people want to stay fully in the world, never waking up, or if they do, only briefly, almost immediately dulled back into a thoughtless existence.

Jesus shows us that there is more to the spiritual journey. This direct confrontation is really just a new beginning in the relationship with God. There are many other holy and positive experiences after this trial. Most spiritual writers become vaguer in their descriptions beyond this point, but they assure us that enduring this trial is worth it, and that life in union with God is the greatest gift and experience a human being can ever have, infinitely surpassing all worldly joys. Most of the miracles we hear of saints doing come later in their spiritual journey, when they are moving into a deeper relationship with God, beyond the stages we can describe.

Many seek spiritual experiences in the world, no longer trusting organized religion. They try to access a glimpse of the direct experience of God seen in the saints' lives: miracles. The problem is that when we seek miracles while still being at the first stage of the spiritual life, while still cabled into the influence of the demons, we are vulnerable to being deceived by them. People usually don't want to devote their lives to seeking God in the spiritual life or even giving Him ten minutes a day in prayer. We usually want miracles on our terms, when we feel out of control and so give a few moments to reflecting on spiritual matters.

In the end it is clear that what is important in all of these cases, in this whole topic, is our relationship with God. It isn't really about what prayers we use, or if we understand the particular ways demons operate. It is about repentance, learning about God, and engaging in a personal relationship with Him. For the Catholic that means participating in the sacramental life, regular sincere prayer, and the spiritual life we have discussed here. Not everyone is called to make that whole journey; we all make it to varying degrees in different areas of our lives and struggles.

In the end, I sincerely hope that you can be encouraged by the reality of the spiritual world to run into the arms of Christ and His Church.

PART II

†

APPENDICES

†

ADAM'S STORY

ONE OF THE FIRST QUESTIONS, if not the first, that I'm asked when I talk with the public is how did you get involved in this? There is a short answer and a long answer. The short answer is that God drew me into this in spite of my broken, sinful nature. The long answer shows how God drew me in, and hopefully addresses the unspoken question: Are you just crazy?

I think there are great dangers of pride and illusions of specialness when talking about one's life. The reasons I want to share this journey are that it points toward the glory of God and the ways God uses us in spite of brokenness and our sinful nature. I have failed in many ways to choose the good, to not be selfish, to be chaste, but I've also tried to commit to doing as much of God's will as I can manage with His grace.

The potentially interesting and "special" experiences I've been able to participate in or witness have nothing to do with my merit, but highlight God giving an interesting life and job to an unworthy and unprofitable servant. My hope is that by sharing this thread of my life I can answer the first question, and allow the reader to judge for themselves about the unspoken one.

EARLY LIFE

I was born in 1970 into a broken family; my parents divorced two weeks after my birth. I was an only child and neither of my parents had other children before or after me. My father was a well-read and intelligent man, but also fairly antisocial when he was young. My mother was bright and well-educated, but was fleeing a family with problems. I got very ill as a newborn, contracting a rare foreign form of influenza that required hospitalization and painful treatment. That was hard on my parents and, presumably, me.

My mother's family was Catholic, going back to Slavic roots. My father's family was ostensibly Lutheran but I never saw them being very religious. I was baptized Catholic and my mother worked as a Catholic grade school teacher when I was an infant. Because she was a single mother and friends with the pastor, Father Martin, he helped her. While my mother worked, his housekeeper cared for me and I practically lived in the rectory for the first six months of my life.

In my early childhood my mother lived with a group of very interesting people in Gradyville, PA. There were about five or six friends of hers of different ethnic and racial backgrounds, and a group of Armenians who lived in the other half of the house. One summer I learned about Native American culture from an Apache Indian (Earnest Victor, an artist) who stayed with us while on tour for his tribe. There was a good bit of space to enjoy nature and the many large parties held there. Living in such a diverse environment in those early years was a great benefit. I felt comfortable with diverse cultures, races, and ethnicities from the very beginning of my life. I don't recall any other children around, so I think I learned how to interact with adults much more than with other children.

Sometime in my early childhood, I started having periodic waking dreams or night terrors. Night terrors occur in stage four sleep when the mind should be mostly shut down. The person often jolts awake with wide eyes, completely terrified. Usually this occurs early in their sleep, maybe within an hour of going to sleep. This panicked state lasts for somewhere around five to twenty minutes. The person doesn't always remember these episodes, but if they do they usually report seeing a figure, person, or animal, and they think that figure intended to hurt them. Sometimes it is snakes or spiders or other animals. Night terrors are different than nightmares in that they continue into the waking state for a number of minutes where you are both still dreaming and partially awake. Night terrors are not uncommon in children, but they only continue into adulthood for about 1 percent of the people who had them as children.

For many, night terrors are triggered by stress in life. Coming from a stoic stock, I think any emotional upset or anxiety about the less-than-perfect parts of life came out when I was sleeping. In my early years this would startle me awake and I would fly out of bed to get away from whatever it was I was seeing and hearing. Over time I became used to this and I would just calmly sit up and look at whatever it was. I think there was a turning point when I once had a strong intuition in my mind during an episode telling me, "You are not to be afraid of this."

These early experiences of waking and hearing or seeing a dream superimposed on reality, with concomitant fear, left me wondering what was happening and what it all meant. As a young person I wasn't aware of the science behind night terrors, they just seemed real at the time.

Now I know that my experiences were typical of people who have night terrors. For me these episodes highlighted the brain's ability to create false experiences.

My grade school and high school experiences were fairly normal, though I was a voracious reader at a young age and so was often bored with school and focused on my own reading and learning outside of class. I worked various part-time jobs and I especially loved the experience of rebuilding the engine of a muscle car in order to learn how motors work.

COLLEGE AND GRADUATE SCHOOL

In college I spent the first two years in the general engineering track where I met my lifelong circle of friends. This was a good foundation in the sciences and gave me a taste of the beauty of mathematics. I moved to Earth science, partially due to my family's business, which was by then a landfill. As an undergrad I worked in a geochemistry laboratory, and some of that research was eventually published. I lived alone during college and focused on school and research, missing out on some of the fun my circle of friends had in a big communal house they rented.

I took some time off from college to work in a high tech instrumentation company where I handcrafted electron beam instruments for a year or so. This taught me about micro-assembly of parts, handcrafting of metals, and very exacting instrumentation standards. It was a good complement to the lessons learned about car engines in my youth. I finished that science degree but I was becoming more interested in psychology as my personal reading broadened.

I reflected on those childhood night terrors and the occasionally recurring waking dreams I was having as an adult and I wanted to understand them. I joined an electroencephalogram (EEG) lab where they use brain wave analysis to infer structure and function of the brain. By making myself useful in that lab and catching up on basic psychology courses, I managed to get a spot in the adult clinical psychology graduate school program at Penn State. As part of the application process, you are interviewed and scrutinized by anywhere from about six to fifteen professors of Clinical Psychology; for me I think it was twelve.

Grad school was an amazing time of learning. The material was challenging and the research end of things was on the edge of what was known. There was a creative interaction with the known science, the data we were getting, and how to analyze it. It was normal for most grad students to work from about 8 or 9 a.m. until 1 a.m. every day. We were required to do a masters paper, a minor project (essentially a second masters in a different area of psychology), comprehensive exams, and then a dissertation. Since we were clinical psychology students, we also worked in the outpatient training clinic for three years learning various approaches to psychological diagnosis, treatment, and assessment.

As part of training to be a therapist, it is normal to get therapy yourself. This teaches you what it is like for the client, as well as helps you with your own issues so they don't interfere with the therapy process for others. I had about two years of individual therapy, as well as maybe a year and half of group therapy with other clinical grad students.

At about the middle of grad school, I met the psychiatrist at the local prison, State Correctional Institution at Rockview. After talking and learning about his work, he thought I should pursue an internship there. After that summer internship they offered me a job and I worked there for about a year and a half (first I was a Psychological Services Associate and then Psychological Services Specialist). It was a *very* strong learning experience. I seemed to have a knack for working with the most violent and/or disturbed inmates. I had a number of intense cases to handle. Psychology staff would also get called to crisis situations regularly; talking a situation down is far better than the risks involved in using force. The full range of serious mental illness was there, concentrated in the special needs block that I was assigned to. That combined with my experience with the intense individual cases led to some confidence in my ability to assist with critical situations. During those years we also had to do hundreds of psychological evaluations for the parole system, providing a solid understanding of various types of personalities and pathologies that lead to bad behavior. After about two years there, it was time to get back to graduate school full time.

I finished a couple of lingering courses, helped with some research projects in the lab, and passed my comprehensive exams. Part of the research in that lab involved hypnosis, which I was interested in. I learned how to hypnotize groups of people and individuals. I only used it clinically twice in my work in the prison and once in the training clinic at Penn State. My Master's degree was on hypnosis and changes in brain waves with shifts in consciousness.

I saw in the lab and in clinical situations that the brain can produce false experiences that seem completely real to the person. Through hypnosis some people can see things that are not there, not see things that are there, completely shut off senses, and produce subjectively real false voices that they can hear. Being able to be hypnotized seems to be genetic; you either are or you are not hypnotizable, and nothing can change it. In the course of my research I got more information on possible answers about my childhood experiences: I learned about sleep paralysis and the two types of sleep-induced hallucinations.

Around that time the paranormal television show craze started. The show *Ghost Hunters* was the first one, a show about two plumbers who were investigating supposed haunting cases in their free time. The case on their first episode was in Altoona, a town about forty-five minutes from where I was at Penn State. I was curious about these people complaining of seeing or hearing ghosts. I wondered if it was a neurological problem, if there was some altered consciousness that allowed imagination to take on a hypnotic character, or if they were undiagnosed, mildly mentally ill. I started researching what I could in the psychological and psychiatric journals but there wasn't much there.

I discovered that one of the few University-based interest groups about the paranormal was right there at Penn State (now there are hundreds of groups but in those days it was very rare). I went to a meeting and a few months later became the staff advisor to the group (a regular requirement of the University for student-interest groups).

Through that group I was able to meet and personally evaluate some people who were complaining of "paranormal" experiences. Over a short time it became clear to me that most people with paranormal complaints are just having false experiences due to sleep disorders, mental or medical illness, medication effects, or aging. This did not however explain all paranormal experiences, particularly those when fully awake, shared by multiple people, or clearly recorded on some form of media.

LESSONS FROM EARLY CASES

When describing a few formative cases that were part of my journey, I will change the identity of the people and the case in order to protect their privacy. The exception to this is the Cranmer case, as this has been publicized in print, television, and movies. There are aspects of some cases I will not describe as they are too horrific and I would never burden the imagination of people by sharing them. Such details can cause fear and in some way gives honor to and celebrates the demons, which is not helpful. There are hundreds of cases, with myriad lessons, but these few are good examples.

It Started With A Bang

One of the first cases I was involved in turned out to be linked to where I am now, over ten years later. There was a case of a haunted house in the Pittsburgh diocese that had been in the local papers twice, with reporters fleeing the house at least once. The couple living there was seeking help. The complaints were of black masses of smoke moving through the house, horrible odors, loud noises, sudden coldness in rooms, being choked and held down, being thrown down the stairs, objects disappearing and re-appearing, and horrible nightmares. I was only one of the people involved in this case, but I will only share my own experiences. This case occurred very early in my career; I was at the stage of interviewing people from a psychological perspective and not yet working for the Church.

I arrived at the case on a sunny summer afternoon. The couple took me through the house and told me about some of the abnormal occurrences and where they happened. When we were on the second floor in the front bedroom, we heard a very loud bang. It seemed to have come from the bathroom, but it was so loud it was hard to tell—it sounded like a pistol being fired indoors. There was nobody else in the house. I checked the bathroom right away and nothing was out of place or broken. The windows were closed. The couple just calmly said, "That's one of the things it does." When I stepped back into the bedroom the temperature had dropped dramatically. There was no air conditioning or explanation for the temperature drop I could see. It felt so cold I was almost surprised I couldn't see my breath.

This same bang had apparently happened at the kitchen table to reporters, who mentioned it in a write up about the house in the paper. A black ball of smoke about fourteen inches around appeared over the middle of the table accompanied by a loud bang that so startled the people they all shot their chairs back from the table. Despite their surprise, the reporters had apparently taken a picture of this ball of black smoke at that moment.

The wife had also taken a series of about six pictures of this black smoke moving across the living room. Normal smoke dissipates and thins out; this stayed together, like a solid mass. In one picture it was in front of a lit lamp and the smoke was solid black over the bright bulb, completely blocking it out.

The husband reported that one night he challenged and mocked whatever was in the house. He said that that night he woke up to something black hovering over him, felt hands like iron grip his neck and choke him, shaking him against the bed. His neck was bruised from this attack, which they had pictures of. He said he had not slept in the bedroom since, only downstairs.

The wife regularly experienced something with no legs pulling itself up to the bed and whispering in her ear when she would be going to sleep. She could never remember what it was saying and very much wanted to be hypnotized to see if that would help her remember. After much consideration and consultation with some people, I agreed to hypnotize her just to see if she could remember these details. There was a concern that this potentially could cause some dramatic reaction or events and so we went to the nearest Catholic Church; it was about 10 p.m. The poor priest who came to the door didn't know what to make of us but gave us holy water and a rosary.

I didn't even get through the hypnotic induction when a different voice spoke out of her and demanded to know what I was doing. What ensued was about three hours of multiple voices coming out of her, mocking us, threatening us, speaking in nonsense, and laughing. One theme they focused on was going up and down the stairs. I've since learned that fallen angels often seem to have a fixation on stairs and water. There are, of course, several biblical references to both stairs and water that are related to angels and fallen angels.

I had no idea how to control the situation, or what to do. Prayer seemed to anger these voices but I didn't know specifically how to use prayer to help. The subject wasn't behaving in a way I had seen before and the normal clinical things you would do to end a hypnotic session had no effect. The voices said they would leave at 3 a.m. by their own choice, which they did. When the woman came out of the trance she said her experience was that she was out of her body and about four feet away watching her body talk to us. She said she could hear multiple evil sounding voices conferring with each other about what to say and do.

I cannot be sure if this was psychosis, a possession state, or a transitory possession state somehow facilitated by the hypnotic trance. I have not used hypnosis since that night—not out of fear; rather, I simply don't see a clinical need for it. I also now know that it is forbidden for Catholics. In the 2003 Church document "Jesus Christ, the Bearer of the Water of Life: A Christian Reflection on the 'New Age,'" promulgated by the Pontifical Council for Culture and the Pontifical Council for Interreligious Dialogue, hypnosis is identified as a New Age technique to "reproduce mystical states at will," creating an atmosphere of psychic weakness and vulnerability.

I never learned what happened to this couple; when trying to check in with them at a later date the new tenant of the home said they had disappeared.

The Cranmer Case

Bob and Lisa Cranmer's home had been worked on by priests in the Pittsburgh diocese for years before I became involved. I was asked to come along with the Penn State group for which I was the staff advisor. The request was to do a fresh evaluation of the situation, specifically psychologically.

The case had started with little things moving and escalated to people being scratched, crucifixes being bent or chewed on, blood spatter marks on walls and clothing, black shadows being seen moving through the house, and horrible odors with no source. All of the family members had experiences in the house; the children basically grew up living with it all.

During the first weekend visit I and others with me saw black shadows I could not explain gliding along the floor, walls, and ceiling. I also experienced a putrid odor that moved like a person walking, leaving no trailing smell behind it. It could be followed through the house by the smell but nothing was visible. I interviewed some of the family members during this first visit and got a sense of their psychological health.

A number of weeks later I was there for another visit. During this visit the priest who had been saying Mass in the house for years and assisting the family was there. That was the first time I witnessed deliverance and exorcism prayers by a priest. That night I was alone reflecting on the case and picturing the house. In my mind's eye I saw the house and saw spirits moving in it. I was surprised by this and shook myself out of my reflection. I went to join the others and shallow scratches formed on my forehead, though I felt nothing. They were photographed while they were there, and they disappeared in about ninety seconds with no trace. They looked like if someone had dragged their fingernails across my forehead hard enough to leave shallow welts.

Eventually, a priest from another diocese came to the house and ended the case with a house exorcism, assisted by a number of other priests. I was not there, though I would meet this priest later, on a dramatic possession case.

First Call To Ministry

About six weeks after the Cranmer case, I got a call requesting I come to a monastery in Pittsburgh for a meeting. I agreed and met with the first priest I had met on the Cranmer case. He said that in prayer they felt there was a place for me in this work. I said yes to him and God. No concrete plans or steps were taken; the plan was to wait on God.

Perseverance In Prayer

Later, while working on another case in Philadelphia, I met the exorcist for that city. After that case was over, this priest asked me to pray with a severe oppression case in his city. Exorcists have to focus on the possession cases and therefore often cannot attend to all demonic oppression cases as well. I prayed with the oppressed man a number of times a week for a year, one or two hours each visit. It was a difficult case that had been going on for over ten years. I learned a lot about prayer in the process of that case. He was delivered three times that year—the deliverance would last for about ten or twenty seconds before he relapsed. At one point, I asked the holy angels to pull a particular demon off of him and I watched him be pulled across the room as if a strong man were pulling a boot off of his foot. His leg was pulled up in the air and his chair was dragged across the room by the force, though I saw nothing there.

Into The Deep Water

Around that time I was put in touch with a different exorcist in a different diocese. I'll never forget the first time we talked. I was handed a phone and he didn't say hello, he just said, "Do you have a wife?" I answered that I didn't. "Do you have children?" he asked. Again, I said no. "Do you have any pets?" he asked. When I confirmed that I didn't, he simply said, "Well, I suppose you can come and talk."

I was not able to visit him right away. A few weeks later on a Saturday morning I woke abruptly out of sleep, sitting bolt upright. For the first time in my life I almost heard a voice in my mind. It said, "Go see the priest." I immediately knew who the voice meant. However, I shrugged this off and lay back down to go back to sleep. A few moments later I almost heard, "I said, go see the priest." This time I froze, becoming slightly nervous. This was a new experience for me. I grabbed my phone and called him, but there was no answer. I thought to myself, *He's not home; it makes no sense to drive all that way. I have no idea if he will be there.* Again, I almost heard in my mind, "He will be there, just go." At this point I had a strong intuition that I should do what this voice was telling me to do. I didn't hear such a clear command again until a few years later during an exorcism with that same priest. It was right both times I experienced it. I drove that day and when I arrived, embarrassed and nervous, I simply said, "Hello, I was sent."

He said, "Well, come in then."

That was the beginning of a great friendship and the biggest learning case of my life so far. He was working on a severe case; it was his first and likely the only case of his life. Six or seven other exorcists had come in from around the world to try and resolve it. The priest who had ended the Cranmer case was consulting on this one also. Over the next few years, I attended well over a hundred exorcisms with that one case alone. We often had exorcism sessions three or four days a week for three or four hours at a time, with frequent crisis calls in the middle of the night to come and calm outbursts that disrupted the home. The possession seemed to stem from a satanic coven but it was impossible to be sure.

One of the many lessons learned in that case was about physical struggle. In the beginning, I would be assigned to just hold one hand or maybe the legs. This meant hours of wrestling and straining, always wary of the possessed getting a hand free, biting my face, or breaking a finger. I was so impressed by the demoniac's strength, and how it never faded, that I thought I should maybe lift weights to get stronger. Then I reflected on this more. Some instinct was telling me it wasn't about the strength in my arms or hands, but rather the strength of my faith.

At the next session, instead of firmly holding that one hand with both of mine in the way I had been shown to do, I gently laid one hand on top of the forearm. As the exorcism started I asked the holy angels to restrain that arm. I wasn't too surprised when the arm didn't move at all; there was no struggle. At the session after that I took it further: I placed two fingers against the arm and asked God to hold it still. All of the struggling was going on for the other people restraining, but the arm I asked God to hold didn't move at all—not even the fingers. At the following session I didn't touch the arm at all, but simply prayed. It didn't move.

There were two firsts during those intensive years of assisting at that exorcism. One was that I saw a ghost in my home, and the other was a disembodied voice.

My home started having a lot of strange phenomenon in that first heavy year: growling in the walls, digital clocks quickly running backwards, black shadow figures standing in the rooms when you woke up in the night, and moments of paralyzing fear as a disembodied demon came into my bedroom. I would always pray, or sometimes jump out of bed startled and swinging, but there was nothing to hit.

At some point in that year, I was sleeping on my couch because my bedroom had too much activity. I was wide awake sitting on the couch wondering if I would get any sleep that night. I was looking at the clock thinking of the exact time. I looked up and I saw a ghost standing in the hall outside of the living room. It was a pale white human figure made of a kind of dim, smoky, liquid light that was gently moving. It looked like my uncle John who had recently died, but younger. I immediately recalled that all the stories say that when you look away and look back the ghost is gone, so I didn't look away.

As I sat there studying this apparition I had plenty of time to note some things. It was a complete human figure, head to toe. It seemed to have clothes on, but it was vague enough I couldn't see their details. The facial figures were not distinct enough to see exactly who it was. The most striking thing though was the nightlight shining on its legs. It was an aqua-colored night light and where it was glowing against the apparition the blue light joined in the pale white of it and gently flowed up its legs like slow moving water. It seemed to flow up to about his upper leg before it diffused into the white of the spirit completely.

After about two minutes, which is an eternity when staring at a ghost, I started to get nervous. Nothing had happened: it didn't move or speak; we just stared at each other. I started to wonder what would happen next as the strangeness of this started to settle in. I looked away to check the time, noting it, and of course when I looked back the spirit was completely gone. That was the first and last time (so far) that I have ever seen a ghost.

My priest friend with whom I was working came and blessed the house, and everything became peaceful there. In those early years I was sure this was spiritual work I was getting involved in, but my personal life was still out of order. I think my sins probably made me vulnerable to those problems, but God limited them and I was never hurt.

After one of the typical draining and difficult nights of exorcism, I was laying down to sleep on my priest friend's couch at the rectory. I was wide awake and reflecting on what had happened that night. As I lay there looking at the ceiling I heard a voice speak from behind my head, maybe a foot away. It spoke audibly in the room; its voice was very deep and gravely. It said, "You won't get me." Doing my best to seem unfazed, I closed my eyes and went to sleep.

Over those first years I became aware that there were very few exorcists, and they were usually alone. There was little communication between them as they were all busy and separated by large distances. Supportive friendships were hard to form. The exorcists were also usually overworked, having a whole diocese or city to take care of.

I got together with the priest I met at the Cranmer case and we decided to put on a conference for exorcists. We recruited a number of the main figures in exorcism and deliverance at that time in the United States. We planned for about a year and had our conference in 2006 in Pittsburgh. It seemed to be a good success. We had brought an exorcist priest from Europe who was our main speaker.

During the conference I had the occasion to walk and talk with our main speaker a number of times. We explored some of the city and talked about many things, particularly mystical theology, the holy angels, and exorcism. By the end of that conference we made plans for me to come to Europe for a visit and train with him.

A few months later I flew to Europe. On the second day of my time there, we started to pray for the first case at his church. We were standing on either side of a man who was sitting in the pew. As he started to shake and manifest, the demon spoke out loudly. It said to me in English, with an American accent, "What are YOU doing here?! Stop that praying; STOP IT!"

Father just looked up at me and raised his eyebrows, and we kept praying. After we were done Father had the man speak to him in his best English, which was halting and with a heavy accent. At the end of that time together, Father said a Mass in Latin in the church for the two of us. We were in his church, which was built in the early 1600s, I think, with just candles. Mass was perhaps two hours, maybe more. I will never forget that Mass; it was a gift from God.

I learned a lot during our time and we had a lot of fun also. I went on to see Father at meetings in Rome and in the States a number of times, and always look forward to a chance to visit again.

Over the next few years, I started working on cases for the Pittsburgh diocese more and more, all house or oppression cases. I continued helping with the severe possession case with my friend and also sometimes travelling to Philadelphia for prayer with the oppression case there.

Through working on cases in a number of dioceses, relationships and connections grew slowly over time. I learned about the International Association of Exorcists in Rome. This is a group of exorcists from all over the world that meet every two years in Italy. By providence one of the people I was working on a case with was on the governing board of the association, so I was able to attend a meeting as an auxiliary member.

The first time I went to the association was amazing. It was a very prayerful, week-long conference with about two hundred priests from many different language groups. The association is the best place to learn from the people with forty-plus years of experience.

The second time I went to the association, I was granted permission to bring a film crew and do interviews for a TV documentary project I wanted to make with the Discovery Channel to counter the poor information being spread by the paranormal television shows. By providence only the first episode, out of eleven, was aired. Though they said they were cancelling the show, they have aired that first episode many times around the world since, and translated it into at least five languages. I think that was the information Jesus wanted to go to the public and it worked out just fine.

About this time I wrapped up graduate school in a sad way. I share this just as the facts of what happened, not out of any anger or negativity. Two weeks before the defense of my dissertation, I had the final meetings with my committee members. One of them asked what I had been up to lately and I said I was doing psychological evaluations for exorcism cases and learning about that ministry. He said, "You have my dream." I had a bad feeling. He went on to say that he was in seminary in the seventies and he left to become a psychologist. His friend in seminary stayed and became a priest, and later an exorcist. It was his dream to do psychological evaluation for exorcism cases, but he was denied by the Church.

The next morning I got a one sentence email from him saying I had to write a sentence for every word in my dissertation. This is, of course, impossible in two weeks and unreasonable in any amount of time. I had to resign from the program as it was not possible to please this committee member. This setback never really affected me though. I was able to go on to work with the most intense and challenging psychological cases in the prisons (where the seriously mentally ill are housed for the most part). My hope is that at some point in life I'll be able to do a dissertation related to my work with the Church.

I continued to work on cases and visit the town where my priest friend lived to help with the exorcisms there. My father came for a visit once and the three of us had a good talk. I recall Father explaining that the exorcism work was very dangerous, and how my father didn't like that.

About a year later I was working on that case and was involved in other possession cases also. My father was at his row house in Philadelphia alone one night. He woke up standing at the top of his stairs, disoriented. The next

thing he knew he was in the air. My father was about 6' 4"
and very strong. He was thrown so hard that he did not
touch the stairs on the way down. He landed at the bottom
and broke his neck. He was spared death and paralysis, but
it took him about two years to recover. His spiritual life
wasn't in order up until then, though the experience mo-
tivated him and it was in a short time. The event made me
think of the early questions about having loved ones. There
is an understanding that the demons will take revenge on
people close to us if they can, since they usually are forbidden to harm those appointed to this ministry.

Looking back I think God allowed that attack on my
father to help him prepare for his death, which would
come soon.

Around 2009 I got a request from the diocese of Tulsa,
Oklahoma, to consult on an exorcism case they had there.
That began a wonderful relationship with the Tulsa diocese.
They have put on national conferences to train exorcists
every year since, and I usually teach or help with questions.
Those conferences prompted me to start working on my
pastoral manual for priests.

The Pittsburgh diocese asked me to move to Pittsburgh
and to work at the chancery starting in July 2014. I agreed,
and moved there about a year before the position started.
I used that time to finally finish my pastoral manual. This
book combined everything I had learned, along with interviews with experienced exorcists. It has been disseminat-
ed freely to all Roman Catholic clergy who wish to have a
copy. I felt a responsibility to write down all of the information God had allowed me to learn from all these unusual
experiences and friendships.

On July 1, 2014, the morning of my first day of work as
a professional religious demonologist, I got a call that my

father was dying. He had gone off his blood thinners for a minor surgery and his irregular heartbeat had caused a clot that went to his brain. By the time I got to him, he could only move his right hand and was on life support. My father died on July 14, 2014. I think it was a good death in that he was blessed and anointed. I said the prayers for the dying for him. I got assurances for forgiveness from everyone I could think of and made sure he was aware of that as best I could.

I do not give the demons credit for my father's accident, or his death that started on the day I started working for the Church. It is Jesus, and not demons, who determine when we are born and when we die.

My Life Now

Since then I have worked full time in this ministry, both on cases and in training priests. By decree of my bishop, I am a Peritus of Religious Demonology and Exorcism, which gives me authority to teach priests on these topics. I continue to consult with priests from all over the country on many cases.

There is nothing special about me; in a sense I have been a spectator as I watch this life unfold in front of me, and I thank God every day for it. I share this story to glorify God and show how He used this unprofitable servant to do His will.

†

SOME LESSONS FROM THE BIBLE

I AM NOT a theologian. These are just some of my personal reflections on the Bible and what we may learn from it in this area.

In Genesis we read the beautiful story of God's creation of the universe. After physical creation is completed Adam and Eve are present in the garden. The very first of God's laws is introduced: Do not eat of the tree of knowledge of good and evil in the middle of the garden.

Into this situation enters the serpent, who was "more subtle than any other wild creature that the LORD God had made" (Gen 3:1). We learn here that Satan was a creature of God. How can this be, since God did not create evil? In order to understand the back story of this creature we must turn from the first book of Scripture to the very last: Revelation.

In chapter 12 of Revelation we read about the war in heaven:

> Now war arose in heaven, Michael and his angels fighting against the dragon; and the dragon and his angels fought, but they were defeated and there was no longer any place for them in heaven. And

the great dragon was thrown down, that ancient serpent, who is called the Devil and Satan, the deceiver of the whole world—he was thrown down to the earth, and his angels were thrown down with him.... "And they have conquered him by the blood of the Lamb and by the word of their testimony, for they loved not their lives even unto death. Rejoice then, O heaven and you that dwell therein! But woe to you, O earth and sea, for the devil has come down to you in great wrath, because he knows that his time is short!" (Rev 12:7–9, 11–12)

This war in heaven starts with the appearance of Mary with child, about to give birth. The next appearance is the Devil who reacts to her by rebelling and causing a third of the angels to rebel with him (stars are symbolic of angels in the Bible). This is a clue that Satan's rebellion involved Mary, which we see repeatedly in the exorcism ministry when he shows great fear and anger whenever Mary is mentioned.

The war in heaven was won by two things: the blood of the Lamb (Jesus' sacrifice) and the testimony of the martyrs (see Rev 12:11). So this battle between spirits with no bodies was a battle of words, followed by the action of Jesus. Michael leads the loyal angels and his name means "who is like God?" This is likely a clue as to the words that defeated Satan. From this it is clear that it is the power of Jesus and positions taken in faith that defeated the Devil.

Satan was cast down to the earth and not into hell. There is a mystery to this. There seems to be a kind of hell damned souls are in, but this isn't yet the lake of fire described at the end of the book of Revelation. From this it has traditionally been concluded that Satan and the fallen angels were cast down to earth. Not only was he clearly cast down to the earth, but the earth and the sea are warned that he has come down to us "in great wrath, because he knows that his time is short!" (Rev 12:12). This is affirmed by Jesus when the seventy-two return rejoicing that the demons they encountered were subject to them because of His name, and He says "I saw Satan fall like lightning from heaven" (Lk 10:18). Peter also warns us to "Be sober, be watchful. Your adversary the devil prowls around like a roaring lion, seeking some one to devour" (1 Pet 5:8).

To sum up the backstory of the snake in the garden of Eden: he was a creature of God who was shown the plan of salvation at the beginning of creation, rebelled over God becoming incarnate through Mary, was cast out of Heaven down to the earth, and now roams here with his other fallen angels until the appointed time of their even greater eternal punishment.

After they were placed in the Garden and were tempted by Satan in the form of the serpent, Adam and Eve disobeyed God by eating the fruit of the Tree of the Knowledge of Good and Evil. They were then cast out of the Garden of Eden to work, toil, and die. The long story of salvation and the repair of this partially broken relationship with God had begun.

The story of human history then develops through a number of books in the Bible, with many instances of temptation and falling to evil being described. We next see the Devil enter the story of salvation in a dramatic way with "a man in the land of Uz, whose name was Job; and that man was blameless and upright, one who feared God, and turned away from evil" (Job 1:1).

A conversation between the Lord and Satan takes place in the first chapter of the Book of Job. The Lord asks

Satan where he has been, and he replies that he has been roaming the earth. The Lord asks him if he has noticed Job, saying there is no one on earth like him. Satan complains that Job is only God-fearing because he has had no hardship and is wealthy. Satan challenges God that if He would remove His protection from his possessions, Job would curse God to his face. What follows are a series of trials Job goes through, each beginning with Satan asking permission from God to visit even greater difficulty and suffering on Job. In the second trial God allows Satan to harm Job's body, but not kill him. A number of Job's friends and family talk to him through the trials, sometimes telling him to give up. Job does complain to God in prayer, but he never rejects God.

In the end the absolute sovereignty of God is reaffirmed and Job confesses that "I know that you can do all things, and that no purpose of yours can be thwarted . . . therefore I despise myself, and repent in dust and ashes" (Job 42:2, 6). God then restores everything to Job, and blesses him with even greater abundance, family, and long years. We see no more mention of the Devil, as he has been defeated by Job who never rejected God and repented.

The Book of Job has two clear lessons: God is all-powerful and cannot be hindered, and the Devil has to ask permission from God for everything that he does. We see that both temptation and trials come from Satan, but it is God's protection and decrees which are important, not the Devil. The Devil is presented as a predictable creature who will always seek to test men and incite rejection of God. People, particularly people the most committed to God, are targeted by the Devil and God allows them to be tested. We see this play out in the life of Job and in the lives of many of the saints, who are often tested fiercely by the Devil as they draw closer to God. The end reward of this struggle is the restoration of all that Satan was allowed to wound, and abundant graces beyond that in the form of an eternal life in heaven with God.

King David cries out in many of the psalms that he is beset by enemies who deny God and seek his destruction. He never gives up on God, but again and again begs God to rise up and assist him. In exorcism work, we see that the psalms cause a particular rage and fear in the demons, likely because they encourage the reader to stay close to God and trust Him.

In the New Testament we get more information about the fallen angels, their condition, and their relationship to Jesus and His followers. There are six major synoptic Gospel accounts of Jesus performing exorcisms, one reference to him casting seven demons out of Mary Magdalene, and a number of Gospel references to Jesus performing many other exorcisms. We also read in the Gospels about Jesus giving authority to the Apostles to cast out demons. The major accounts are:

- Jesus exorcising a man possessed by an unclean spirit in the Synagogue in Capernaum (Mk 1:23–28, Lk 4:33–37).
- Jesus exorcising the Gerasene man possessed by "Legion" (Mk 5:1–20, Mt 8:28–34, Lk 8:26–39).
- Jesus exorcising the man made dumb and blind by a demon (Mt 9:32–33, Mt 12:22–23, Lk 11:14).
- Jesus exorcising the daughter of a Gentile woman (Mt 15:21–28, Mk 7:24–30).
- Jesus exorcising the boy possessed by a demon (Mt 17:14–21, Mk 9:14–29, Lk 9:27–49).
- Jesus exorcising a man possessed by a demon that

made him mute, followed by a blind man (Mt 9:32–34).

Other references to exorcism ministry in the Gospels are:

- Jesus' healings and exorcisms (Mk 1:32–34, Mt 8:16–17, Lk 4:40–41).
- Jesus preaching and casting out demons in Galilee (Mk 1:39, Mt 4:23, and Lk 4:44).
- Jesus silencing a demon that recognized Him (Mk 3:11, Mt 12:15–16, and Lk 4:41).
- The Apostles casting out many demons (Mk 6:13).
- Jesus healing a crippled woman bound by Satan for eighteen years (Lk 13:10–17).
- Jesus casting seven demons out of Mary Magdalene (Mk 16:9 and Lk 8:2).

The issue of authority over demons is important and is shown in a number of places. We read about Jesus sending the Twelve Apostles out two by two and giving them authority over impure spirits (see Mk 6:7, Mt 10:8, Lk 9:1). This highlights that the full authority to cast out demons resides with the Apostles and the successors of the Apostles today. We also read of the seventy disciples of Jesus who cast out demons in Jesus' name (Lk 10:17–18). Finally, we read about the itinerant Jewish exorcists who experiment by trying to exorcise a demon by saying, "I adjure you by the Jesus whom Paul preaches" (Acts 19:13). The evil spirit replies, "Jesus I know, and Paul I know; but who are you?" (Acts 19:15). The possessed man then overcomes them and these exorcists end up fleeing naked and wounded. These stories show us that the Apostles have the full authority themselves, the disciples can command in the name of Jesus, but people without a personal relationship with Jesus cannot use his name like a magic word.

An interesting story that seems to stand in contrast to the itinerant Jewish exorcists is that of the man who was casting out demons in Jesus' name but not following the Apostles (Mark 9:38–39). The Apostles tell Jesus about this man and Jesus replies to not prevent him because "no one who does a mighty work in my name will be able soon after to speak evil of me. For he that is not against us is for us" (Mk 9:40). Since miracles were performed to demonstrate the truth of the Gospel being preached, we may conclude that this man was preaching the Gospel of Jesus Christ. There may be more to the situation—perhaps this man was associated with Jesus previously and the Twelve did not know him. Any doubt about who can do exorcisms today is removed by canon law: only a priest with permission from his bishop can perform a solemn exorcism.

At the start of his public ministry, Jesus went to visit His cousin John and be baptized. At His baptism the Spirit of God descended on Him like a dove and those present heard "a voice from heaven, saying, 'This is my beloved Son, with whom I am well pleased'" (Mt 3:17). The very next verse after God confirms Jesus as His son in this beautiful scene, we read, "Then Jesus was led by the Spirit into the wilderness to be tempted by the devil" (Mt 4:1).

There are many mysteries in the temptation of Jesus. It may be implied that Satan wasn't completely sure who Jesus was, starting his first temptation with "If you are the Son of God . . ." (Mt 4:3). This may be a reminder that Satan's mind is limited, and that God can limit his knowledge. If Satan was sure this was God, why would be try to tempt Him at all? We know from the book of Job that Satan was used to speaking to God on occasion, but in those instances he clearly knew his place and only made requests, not challenges.

When tempted to make bread from the stones to feed himself Jesus replies by quoting Scripture, saying that we live from every word that comes from the mouth of God, and not by bread alone (see Mt 4:4, Lk 4:4). In a way, this echoes and rebukes Satan's first temptation to Eve to eat something.

Satan then tries to flip this against Jesus by quoting Scripture to Him and saying his angels will support Him if He falls. This shows that Satan knows Scripture well and he is clever enough to use it as a temptation. Jesus responds in an interesting way, perhaps implying that He is God, or that by testing the angels one is testing God's promise. He says "Again it is written, 'You shall not tempt the Lord your God'" (Mt 4:7, cf. Lk 4:12).

Finally, Satan takes Jesus to a high mountain and offers Him all the kingdoms of the world if Jesus will worship him. This time Satan doesn't say "If you are the son of God." Satan knows at least some of the plan of God; he knows that the son of God is destined to rule the world with an iron rod. This is perhaps a final test, and an attempt to derail Jesus' mission by giving Him the world now and fulfilling that part of the plan in a perverted way. Jesus replies, "It is written, 'You shall worship the Lord your God, and him only shall you serve'" (Lk 4:8; cf. Mt 4:10), and the Devil leaves Him.

There are many deep lessons in the temptations of Jesus but these are the basic ones: resist temptation using Scripture, do not test God, and follow the First Commandment.

In Mark's Gospel, Jesus is baptized and then He calls His disciples. The first thing He does is teach in the synagogue at Capernaum where He also performs an exorcism. There was a possessed man there and the demons exclaimed, "What have you to do with us, Jesus of Nazareth? Have you come to destroy us? I know who you are, the Holy One of God!" (Mk 1:24). Jesus tells them to be quiet and simply commands them to come out. This is a good lesson for us, as Jesus did not waste any time talking with the demons, or even responding to them. The fact that He simply said, "Come out of him!" and they obeyed caused Jesus' fame to "spread everywhere throughout the whole surrounding region of Galilee" (Mk 1:28). The people reacted to His new teaching with authority and Jesus' power to command unclean spirits. If Jesus' first recorded miracle in the Gospel of Mark was an exorcism, it doesn't seem unreasonable that He would still use exorcisms today to remind the world of who He is. Later in Mark when Jesus appoints the Twelve Apostles, their mission is to preach and drive out demons, exactly as Jesus did first in Capernaum (Mk 3:13–19).

Possibly the most famous exorcism Jesus did was of the Gerasene demoniac, recounted later in Mark 5:1-20 and also in Matthew and Luke. Jesus and His followers crossed over to the territory of the Gerasenes and as soon as Jesus got out of the boat this possessed man met Him. The man was living among tombs and was too strong for people, or even shackles and chains, to restrain. He prostrated himself before Jesus as Jesus commanded the spirits to come out of him. The man was "crying out with a loud voice . . . 'What have you to do with me, Jesus, Son of the Most High God? I adjure you by God, do not torment me" (Mk 5:7).

It seems that these demons didn't come out at the first command, since the Gospel says Jesus was commanding them to leave when the man begged Jesus to not torment him. So, Jesus does something different from His first exorcism: He demands information. "And Jesus asked him, 'What is your name?' He replied, 'My name is Legion; for we are many'" (Mk 5:9). The demons pleaded to not be sent out of that territory, which is interesting. They asked to go into a herd of about two thousand swine (a Roman-legion size varied over the history of Rome, but was about five thousand soldiers). The Gospel says Jesus let them, which shows that Jesus has authority over not just a demon leaving a person, but where it goes once cast out. This also shows that demons can possess animals, which has been seen in cases from time to time. The pigs ran into the sea and died, angering the local people and inciting them to beg Jesus to leave their territory . . . which is probably what the demons wanted.

Later in Mark, Jesus is visited by a Greek woman in Tyre, pleading for Him to help her possessed daughter. Jesus first refuses, saying, "Let the children first be fed, for it is not right to take the children's bread and throw it to the dogs" (Mk 7:27). She replies that even the dogs under the table eat the children's scraps. Jesus says that she may go home, that the demon had left her daughter. This shows that a direct confrontation with a possessed person is not always needed; Jesus frees some people who simply ask Him as an intercession. This is helpful and encourages a focus on God and prayer, not just a focus on the "magic" of having an exorcism done.

In the eleventh chapter of Luke, Jesus is driving out a demon that was causing muteness in a person. After He does this He reveals by what power He is driving out demons. Some of the people said He was driving out demons by the power of Beelzebul—essentially accusing Him of using a demon to drive out a demon. Jesus explains that Satan's kingdom cannot work against itself and stay strong. He poses an interesting question, asking by whom their people drive out demons. This hints that exorcism was part of the general culture at the time. Jesus then says something powerful: "If it is by the finger of God that I cast out demons, then the kingdom of God has come upon you" (Lk 11:20).

Jesus then warns the people about unclean spirits returning after a person is exorcised. This seems to be related to the state of people who have not invited God into their hearts as the new "strong man" of their house, making them safe from a return of the unclean spirits.

In Mark 9:14–29 the interesting story of a possessed boy is presented. The description sounds like epileptic seizures, and the boy is noted as being deaf and mute also. Jesus' disciples had tried to exorcise the boy, but failed. The father of the boy describes the fits the boy has and asks Jesus, "If you can do anything, have pity on us and help us" (Mk 9:22). Jesus points to the serious error in this: "If you can! All things are possible to him who believes" (Mk 9:23). When Jesus commands the mute and deaf spirit to come out, He gives an additional command this time: "and never enter him again!" (Mk 9:25). When the disciples ask Jesus why they were not able to do the exorcism he says, "This kind can only come out through prayer" (Mk 9:29). The United States Catholic Conference of Bishops notes, "Some manuscripts add, 'But this kind does not come out except by prayer and fasting'; this is a variant of the better reading of Mk 9:29."[8]

There are many lessons in this story. Jesus shows that what may look like a medical problem may in fact be

---

8 http://www.usccb.org/bible/matthew/17#48017021-1.

spiritual, but we should never eschew medical treatment because we think a problem is spiritual. He also teaches us that some spirits require different amounts of prayer (or fasting) to cast out.

In Matthew 8:16–17, Mark 1:32-34, and Luke 4:40–41, Jesus is described as performing many exorcisms at sunset. In Luke it is noted that the demons were trying to call out that He was the Son of God, but Jesus would not let them speak. Few details are given in these accounts. The emphasis seems to be on Jesus' compassion for the masses, because all were either healed or exorcised that came Him that day. This is perhaps a reminder that the love and compassion of Jesus is there for all the people afflicted by illness or demons, not just some.

†

PRAYERS

THE LITANY OF THE SAINTS

V. Lord, have mercy on us.

R. Christ, have mercy on us.

V. Lord, have mercy on us.

V. Christ, hear us.

R. Christ, graciously hear us.

V. God the Father of heaven,

R. Have mercy on us.

V. God the Son, Redeemer of the world,

R. Have mercy on us.

V. God the Holy Spirit,

R. Have mercy on us.

V. Holy Trinity, one God,

R. Have mercy on us.

V. Holy Mary,

R. Pray for us. *(common response)

V. Holy Mother of God, *

V. Holy Virgin of virgins, *

V. Saint Michael, *

V. Saint Gabriel, *

V. Saint Raphael, *

V.   All ye holy Angels and Archangels, *

V.   All ye holy orders of blessed Spirits, *

V.   Saint John the Baptist, *

V.   Saint Joseph, *

V.   All ye holy Patriarchs and Prophets, *

V.   Saint Peter, *

V.   Saint Paul, *

V.   Saint Andrew, *

V.   Saint James, *

V.   Saint John, *

V.   Saint Thomas, *

V.   Saint James, *

V.   Saint Philip, *

V.   Saint Bartholomew, *

V.   Saint Matthew, *

V.   Saint Simon, *

V.   Saint Thaddeus, *

V.   Saint Matthias, *

V.   Saint Barnabas, *

V.   Saint Luke, *

V.   Saint Mark, *

V.   All ye holy Apostles and Evangelists, *

V.   All ye holy Disciples of the Lord, *

V.   All ye Holy Innocents, *

V.   Saint Stephen, *

V.   Saint Lawrence, *

V.   Saint Vincent, *

V.   Saints Fabian and Sebastian, *

V.   Saints John and Paul, *

V.   Saints Cosmas and Damian, *

V.   Saints Gervase and Protase, *

V.   All ye holy martyrs, *

V.   Saint Sylvester, *

V. Saint Gregory, *

V. Saint Ambrose, *

V. Saint Augustine, *

V. Saint Jerome, *

V. Saint Martin, *

V. Saint Nicholas, *

V. All ye holy bishops and confessors, *

V. All ye holy doctors, *

V. Saint Anthony, *

V. Saint Benedict, *

V. Saint Bernard, *

V. Saint Dominic, *

V. Saint Francis, *

V. All ye holy priests and levites, *

V. All ye holy monks and hermits, *

V. Saint Mary Magdalen, *

V. Saint Agatha, *

V. Saint Lucy, *

V. Saint Agnes, *

V. Saint Cecilia, *

V. Saint Catherine, *

V. Saint Anastasia, *

V. All ye holy virgins and widows.*

V. All ye Holy Saints of God,

R. Make intercession for us.

V. Be merciful,

R. Spare us, O Lord.

V. Be merciful,

R. Graciously hear us, O Lord.

V. From all evil,

R. O Lord, deliver us. *

V. From all sin,

V. From Thy wrath,

V. From a sudden and unprovided death,

V. From the snares of the devil,

V. From anger, and hatred, and all ill will,

V. From the spirit of fornication,

V. From lightning and tempest,

V. From the scourge of earthquake,

V. From plague, famine, and war,

V. From everlasting death,

V. Through the mystery of Thy holy Incarnation,

V. Through Thy coming,

V. Through Thy Nativity,

V. Through Thy baptism and holy fasting,

V. Through Thy Cross and Passion,

V. Through Thy death and burial,

V. Through Thy holy Resurrection,

V. Through Thine admirable Ascension,

V. Through the coming of the Holy Spirit, the Paraclete,

V. In the day of judgment,

R. We sinners, We beseech Thee, hear us. *

V. That Thou wouldst spare us,

V. That Thou wouldst pardon us,

V. That Thou wouldst bring us to true penance,

V. That Thou wouldst vouchsafe to preserve our Apostolic Prelate and all orders of the Church in holy religion,

V. That Thou wouldst vouchsafe to humble the enemies of holy Church,

V. That Thou wouldst vouchsafe to give peace and true concord to Christian kings and princes,

V. That Thou wouldst vouchsafe to grant peace and unity to the whole Christian world,

V. That Thou wouldst restore to the unity of the

Church all who have strayed from the truth, and lead all unbelievers to the light of the Gospel,

V. That Thou wouldst vouchsafe to confirm and preserve us in thy holy service,

V. That Thou wouldst lift up our minds to heavenly desires,

V. That Thou wouldst render eternal blessings to all our benefactors,

V. That Thou wouldst deliver our souls and the souls of our brethren, relatives, and benefactors from eternal damnation,

V. That Thou wouldst vouchsafe to give and preserve the fruits of the earth,

V. That Thou wouldst vouchsafe to grant eternal rest to all the faithful departed,

V. That Thou wouldst vouchsafe graciously to hear us,

V. Son of God,

V. Lamb of God, Who takest away the sins of the world,

R. Hear us, O Lord.

V. Lamb of God, Who takest away the sins of the world,

R. Graciously hear us, O Lord.

V. Lamb of God, Who takest away the sins of the world,

R. Have mercy on us.

V. Christ, hear us,

R. Christ, graciously hear us.

V. Lord, have mercy on us,

R. Christ, have mercy on us.

V. Lord, have mercy on us.

ABBREVIATED OFFICE FOR THE DEAD[9]

Lesson IX

Job 10:18-22

Why didst thou bring me forth out of the womb? O that I had been consumed that eye might not see me! I should have been as if I had not been, carried from the womb to the grave. Shall not the fewness of my days be ended shortly? Suffer me, therefore, that I may lament my sorrow a little. Before I go, and return no more to a land that is dark and covered with the mist of death; a land of misery and darkness, where the shadow of death, and no order, but everlasting horror dwelleth.

Responsory I

From the pathways of hell, deliver me, O Lord, Who didst break the gates of brass asunder, Who didst descend into limbo and grant the souls therein light, that they who were in affliction and darkness might behold Thee.

V. They cried out, saying: Thou hast come, O our Redeemer!
R. They who were in affliction and in darkness.
V. Eternal rest grant unto them, O Lord. And let perpetual light shine upon them.
R. Who were in affliction and in darkness.

---

9 From the old Roman Ritual Volume II, trans. Weller, found in footnote no. 2.

Psalm 146 [145]

Praise the Lord, O my soul! My lifelong I will praise the Lord, I will sing to my God till my last breath. Put not your trust in princes, in mere man with no power to save, his breath gone, he returns into dust: then all his projects perish. Happy he whose helper is the God of Jacob, whose hope is in the Lord, his God, Who made heaven and earth and the sea and all therein, Who keeps faith forever, renders justice to the oppressed, gives bread to the hungry. The Lord gives release to the captives, the Lord opens the eyes of the blind. The Lord raises up them that are bowed down, the Lord loves the righteous. The Lord watches over strangers, He supports the orphan and the widow, but He confounds the designs of the wicked. The Lord shall reign forever; thy God, O Sion, reigns for ages and ages.

Eternal rest grant unto them, O Lord. And let perpetual light shine upon them.

V. From the gates of hell.
R. Deliver his (her) soul (their souls), O Lord.
V. May he (she) (they) rest in peace.
R. Amen.
V. O Lord, hear my prayer.
R. And let my cry come unto Thee.
V. The Lord be with you.
R. And with thy spirit.

Psalm 116 [114]

I love the Lord because He hath heard my voice and supplication, and hath bent toward me His ear on the day that I cried out to him. The fetters of death encompassed me and the snares of the netherworld gripped me, anguish and grief overtook me. Then I called on the name of the Lord: "O Lord, save my life!"

The Lord is gracious and just, and compassionate is our God. The Lord it is Who guards simple hearts; I was wretched, and He saved me. Return then, my soul unto thy peace, for the Lord hath dealt kindly with thee. For he hath snatched my soul from death, banished my tears, kept my feet from stumbling. I will walk before the Lord in the land of the living.

Eternal rest grant unto them, O Lord. And let perpetual light shine upon them.

> Antiphon: I will walk before the Lord in the land of the living.
> Our Father (inaudibly until)
> V. And lead us not into temptation.
> R. But deliver us from evil.

O God, Whose nature it is ever to have mercy and to spare, humbly we beseech Thee on behalf of the soul of Thy servant, N. (Thy handmaid, N.), whom Thou hast now called out of this world. Deliver not his (her) soul into the hands of the enemy, and forget him (her) not forever, but command that he (she) be received by the holy angels and taken into the heavenly fatherland. Thus let him (her) who believed in Thee and hoped in Thee be spared the sufferings of hell's punishment, and come into possession of joys everlasting. Through our Lord Jesus Christ, Thy Son, Who liveth and reigneth with Thee in the unity of the Holy Spirit, God, for all eternity. R. Amen.

This paragraph only for priests and bishops:
[O God, in raising Thy servants to the dignity of a bishop or priest, Thou hast established them in the ranks of the priesthood of Thine Apostles; thus grant, we pray Thee, that they may likewise be enrolled in their company in heaven.]

O God, the Creator and Redeemer of all the faithful, grant to the souls of Thy servants and handmaids forgiveness of all their sins. And by our loving entreaties let them obtain the pardon they have ever longed for. Thou Who livest and reignest with God the Father in the unity of the Holy Spirit, God, forever and evermore. R. Amen.

V. Eternal rest grant unto them, O Lord.
R. And let perpetual light shine upon them.
V. May they rest in peace.
R. Amen.

Responsory

O Lord, when Thou shalt come to judge the world, where will I hide myself from the face of Thy wrath? For I have sinned exceedingly in my life.

V. I have dread for my sins, I blush before Thee;
   when Thou shalt come, condemn me not.
R. For I have sinned exceedingly in my life.

Psalm 23 [22]

The Lord is my Shepherd, and I lack nothing; He maketh me encamp in green pastures. He leadeth me to water beside which I can rest; He renewed my spirits. He guidest me on right paths for His name's sake. Even though I enter a valley of shadows, I will fear no evil, for thou art with me. Thy rod and thy staff, they give me confidence. Thou dost spread for me a banquet in sight of envious oppressors. Thou annointest my head with oil; my cup overflows. Goodness and favor shall follow me all the days of my life. And I will dwell in the house of the Lord for length of days.

Eternal rest grant unto them, O Lord. And let perpetual light shine upon them.

Antiphon: Remember not, O Lord, the frailties of my youth nor later offenses.

Psalm 25 [24]

To Thee, O Lord God, I lift up my soul. In Thee I put my trust; let me not be confounded, let not mine enemies exult over me. Since none that hopes in Thee shall be confounded; but they shall be foiled who lightly break faith with Thee. Show me, O Lord, thy ways, and teach me thy paths. Guide me in thy truth and instruct me, for thou art the God of my salvation in Whom I trust always. Be mindful, O Lord, of thine acts of compassion and of thy mercies of long ago. Remember not the frailties of my youth nor my later offenses; but be mindful of me in thy kindness, for the sake of thy goodness, O Lord.

Antiphon to the Canticle of Zachary

I am the Resurrection and the life; he that believeth in me, although he be dead, shall live; and every one that liveth and believeth in me shall not die forever.

Canticle of Zachary (Luke 1:68-79)

Blessed be the Lord God of Israel, for He hath visited and redeemed His people. And hath raised up a mighty Savior for us in the lineage of David His servant.

Thus He foretold by the mouth of His holy prophets who have been from times ancient; that He might rescue us from our enemies—from the hand of all that hate us. Now is granted the mercy promised to our fathers, remembering His holy covenant; and the oath which He swore to Abraham our father that He would extend to us; that we, delivered from the hand of our enemies, might serve Him without fear, Living in holiness and righteousness before Him all our days. And thou, child, shall be called the prophet of the Highest, for thou shalt go before the face of the Lord to prepare his ways; to give knowledge of salvation to His people—the remission of their sins, through the bounteous mercy of our God in which the Orient from on high hath visited us, to give light to them that sit in darkness and in the shadow of death, to direct our feet into the way of peace. Eternal rest grant unto them, O Lord. And let perpetual light shine upon them.

Antiphon: I am the Resurrection and the life; he that believeth in me, although he be dead, shall live; and every one that liveth and believeth in me shall not die forever.

Hereupon all kneel for the prayers:

Our Father (inaudibly until)

V. And lead us not into temptation.

R. But deliver us from evil.

THE MAGNIFICAT

My soul proclaims the greatness of the Lord, my spirit rejoices in God my Savior for he has looked with favor on his lowly servant. From this day all generations will call me blessed: the Almighty has done great things for me, and holy is his Name.

He has mercy on those who fear him in every generation. He has shown the strength of his arm, he has scattered the proud in their conceit.

He has cast down the mighty from their thrones, and has lifted up the lowly. He has filled the hungry with good things, and the rich he has sent away empty.

He has come to the help of his servant Israel for he remembered his promise of mercy, the promise he made to our fathers, to Abraham and his children forever.

PRAYER TO SAINT MICHAEL THE ARCHANGEL

St. Michael the Archangel, defend us in battle; be our protection against the wickedness and snares of the devil. May God rebuke him, we humbly pray.

And do thou, O prince of the heavenly host, by the power of God cast into hell Satan and all of the evil spirits who prowl about the world seeking the ruin of souls.

Amen.

RENUNCIATIONS

N. Do you renounce any ties to the devil established through . . .

The occult
Casting spells
Divination
Consulting psychics
Mediumship

Praying to idols
Making deals with spirits
Inviting spirits to manifest or communicate
Inviting spirits to touch you
Multi-generational sin
Consecration to the devil by ancestors
Owning cursed objects
Black magic used against you
Unconfessed sin
Drug use
Alcohol abuse
Being a willing witness to magic
Any other ways?

N. Please say 'Jesus, please help me with this spiritual problem and break these ties.'

Lord Jesus Christ, please break all rights the devil has to N. based on these things they have renounced.

Renewal of baptismal promises

V. Do you reject Satan?
R. I do.

V. And all his works?
R. I do.

V. And all of his empty promises?
R. I do.

V. Do you believe in God, the Father Almighty, creator of heaven and earth?
R. I do.

V. Do you believe in Jesus Christ, his only Son, our Lord, who was born of the Virgin Mary was crucified, died, and was buried, rose from the dead, and is now seated at the right hand of the Father?

R. I do.

V. Do you believe in the Holy Spirit, the holy Catholic Church, the communion of saints, the forgiveness of sins, the resurrection of the body, and life everlasting?

R. I do.

V. God, the all-powerful Father of our Lord Jesus Christ has given us a new birth by water and the Holy Spirit, and forgiven all our sins. May he also keep us faithful to our Lord Jesus Christ for ever and ever.

R. Amen.

†

GLOSSARY

Angels – Immortal spiritual beings with free will created by God before physical creation. The angels were shown what their function was in God's plan. The angels that chose to obey God were granted the beatific vision. Angels do not have physicality or locality in space the way living humans do. For instance, Saint Michael the Archangel may respond to prayers in many locations at the same time, while simultaneously being in the presence of God.

Beatific vision – Being in the presence of, and seeing, God. The obedient holy angels received the beatific vision after their choice to obey. Human souls hope to receive the beatific vision after their particular judgement, or after the general judgement.

Damned souls – Souls that were damned at their particular judgement. These souls become, in a sense, the property of Satan. Damned souls are usually only encountered during solemn exorcisms of people. In those instances they are almost always the souls of people that contributed to the possession of the person being exorcised.

Demons (Fallen Angels) – The angels that chose to reject the ministry they were created for. These angels never received the beatific vision but were cast out of heaven and down to Earth. They cannot repent and become holy angels because their choice was made with a complete understanding of the consequences. In addition, they do not wish to repent but are consumed with hatred of God and of the people created in the image of God. There are demons who fell from each choir of angels and so there is a hierarchy of demons under Satan.

Deprecatory prayer – Prayer that is a request to God to assist with something. When this request is to free a person of a spiritual problem, it may be referred to as deliverance, or deliverance prayer.

Exorcism – An action of the Church that includes a command for demons to leave a person, location, or object. An exorcism can be minor or solemn.

First class relics – A physical part of the body of a saint. A living person is a body and soul united in life. The body of a dead saint continues to be part of the whole person until the Final Judgement, when body and soul are reunited (their body will be then be glorified and so immortal and changed). First class relics are therefore part of a whole person who is in the face-to-face presence with God. Because of this, graces are conveyed by first class relics when the intercession of that Saint is requested. These graces have taken the form of physical healings, spiritual healings, and myriad other forms of assistance from God. First class relics are commonly used in exorcism work because the demons are significantly affected by the first class relics of Saints, whom they greatly fear.

General judgement – Jesus will return and judge every human and angel at the end of time. Souls will be reunited with their now glorified body before they are judged as a whole person. The Devil, the angels that rebelled with him, and the people that are damned will be thrown into the lake of fire. Those already in heaven with Jesus will remain in that condition; they cannot lose heaven. Those in purgatory will go to heaven.

Heaven – Eternally experiencing God directly.

Holy angels – The angels that chose to be obedient to God at the beginning of creation. They cannot rebel against God because they have received the beatific vision and experience God directly for eternity. They are simultaneously in the presence of God and performing their appointed tasks in creation. (Matthew 18:10—"See that you do not despise one of these little ones; for I tell you that in heaven their angels always behold the face of my Father who is in heaven.")

Imprecatory prayer – Prayer that is a direct command to a demon in the name of Jesus. Prayers against demons that include imprecatory commands (the minor and solemn exorcisms and Baptism) are reserved to priests.

Minor exorcism (also: Leonine exorcism, "Chapter 3") – A deliverance rite intended for places where the activity of the Devil is suspected, not for possessed people. Pope Leo XIII wrote the minor exorcism, and it was included as an appendix to the solemn exorcism in the Roman Ritual. It cannot be said by lay people; it can only be said by priests. There are some websites and phone apps that incorrectly instruct laity to use this prayer. The minor exorcism includes an imprecatory command.

Particular judgement – At the moment of death each person participates in their particular judgement by God, which is based on the Ten Commandments and (for Catholics) obedience to the Precepts of the Church. This judgement immediately leads to heaven, purgatory, or hell. If a person is baptized and does not have unconfessed mortal sin on their soul, they either go to heaven or purgatory. In the case of an unbaptized person with no mortal sin on their soul, the mercy of God is presumed. Though Confession removes mortal sin from the soul, there is still a time of purification for that sin in purgatory. This is not a punishment for that sin but a restoring of the diminishment of that person caused by their sin. If a person has unconfessed mortal sin on their soul, they go to hell. Mortal sins are intentional violations of the precepts of the Church or the Ten Commandments.

Poor souls (Also: souls in purgatory, "ghosts") – Souls in purgatory are sometimes allowed to petition the living for prayers or sacrifices to hasten their purgation. This usually happens with the saints but can happen to anyone. Usually there is an appearance or manifestation that implies the identity of the soul. These manifestations are non-destructive and not inherently terrifying. The poor souls do not have conversations with the living; they only signal a need for prayer, nothing more. Conversation draws a person into violation of the First Commandment because it provides information or comfort from a spirit other than God.

Purgatory – Being purified of the temporal component associated with confessed sins. This process can be hastened by the prayers and sacrifices of the living offered for the remission of the temporal component of sin.

Saints – Human beings who have died and are now in the presence of God. They were either judged to be worthy of the beatific vision at their death, or have completed the expiation of the temporal component of their sins in purgatory. Because saints are in the presence of God, we can ask them to pray for us to God—to intercede on our behalf. We can only publicly venerate saints whom the Church has canonized (declared to be saints). We may privately ask those whom we presume are saints with God, but have not been publicly canonized by the Church, for their intercession.

Second class relics – A physical object that was in contact with a saint when they were alive, usually something they owned such as a book, a rosary, or clothing. Second class relics can have the same effect as first class relics, particularly relics of the True Cross of Jesus Christ, which have produced many miracles.

Solemn exorcism – The rite of the Church used to assist people who are possessed by demons. Solemn exorcisms may only be performed by a priest with permission from their bishop. The solemn exorcism for people was revised in 1999 as part of the Second Vatican Council.

The Precepts of the Church – The Precepts of the Church are assumed to be followed in the context of a moral life. They are: attending Mass on Sundays and days of obligation, Confession at least once a year, receiving Communion at least once during the Easter season, observing days of fasting and abstinence, and helping to provide for the needs of the Church.

The Ten Commandments – 1. I am the LORD your God: you shall not have strange Gods before Me. 2. You shall not take the name of the LORD your God in vain. 3. Remember to keep holy the LORDS Day. 4. Honor your father and your mother. 5. You shall not kill. 6. You shall not commit adultery. 7. You shall not steal. 8. You shall not bear false witness against your neighbor. 9. You shall not covet your neighbor's wife. 10. You shall not covet your neighbor's goods.

Third class relics – Something touched to a first class relic. Third class relics also convey grace, and miracles have been associated with them. In the Early Church all relics were linen cloth which had been left in the tombs of saints for a time. It was only later that second and first class relics came into use.

†

SUGGESTED READING

THERE ARE relatively few authoritative books on the topics of possession, exorcism, deliverance, and hauntings. These will provide the interested reader a full enough treatment to have a working vocabulary and basic understanding of the principles. It must be understood that much of our knowledge of the actual process of exorcism is passed down through a verbal tradition in the context of mentorship relationships and in internal materials that are not published. Reading in the public domain is not adequate training to safely interact with demons directly.

I have a pastoral manual for priests addressing all of the case types referenced here. It will be sent free to Roman Catholic clergy upon request. My email is ablai@diopitt.org and my website for the public is www.religious-demonology.com.

Amorth, Gabriele. *An Exorcist Explains the Demonic: The Antics of Satan and His Army of Fallen Angels.* Edited by Stefano Stimamiglio, translated by Charlotte J. Fasi. Manchester, NH: Sophia Institute Press, 2016.
This recent book published by Father Amorth, the

former president of the International Association of Exorcists, is the best treatment of this topic in English.

————. *An Exorcist Tells His Story*. San Francisco: Ignatius Press, 1999.

This book has become a classic in the field. It has the Nihil Obstat and Imprimatur. Father Amorth is probably the most well-known exorcist in the world. This book conveys lessons learned in a lifetime of experience as an exorcist.

————. *An Exorcist: More Stories* San Francisco: Ignatius Press, 2002.

In this book Fr. Amorth sheds light on the occult origin of many of the cases. It has the Nihil Obstat and Imprimatur.

Balducci, Corrado. *The Devil: "...alive and active in our world."* Translated and adapted by Jordan Aumann, O.P. New York: Alba House, 1990.

This book gives a broad treatment to spiritual problems and gives a good framework for understanding them and their treatment. It has the Nihil Obstat and Imprimatur.

Bamonte, Francesco. *Diabolical Possession and Exorcism: How to Recognize the Shrewd Deceiver.* ISBN 978-978-087-255-7.

This book by the current president of the International Association of Exorcists is in English. It has the Nihil Obstat and Imprimatur. It gives a rare window into the knowledge of one of our elders in the global exorcist community.

The Bible

The Gospels of Matthew, Mark, Luke, and John provide many examples of how to deal with demons. Revelation describes the war in heaven and the fall of some of the angels. Job illustrates the subservience of Satan to the Lord and that Satan's actions are only with permission from God. I suggest the New American Bible, Revised Edition, from Saint Benedict Press.

Lozano, Neal. *Unbound: A Practical Guide to Deliverance.* Grand Rapids, MI: Chosen Books, 2010.

This book provides good insight into the inner healing aspects of deliverance ministry: repentance, renunciation, and forgiveness.

MacNutt, Francis. *Deliverance from Evil Spirits: A Practical Manual.* Grand Rapids, MI: Chosen Books, 2009.

This book conveys both a broad understanding of deliverance ministry and the practical details of how to do it.

Scanlan, T.O.R, Michael and Randall Cirner. *Deliverance from Evil Spirits: A Weapon for Spiritual Warfare.* Ann Arbor, MI: Servant Books, 1980.

This book on deliverance is by one of the spiritual fathers of the Charismatic Movement in the United States. Father Scanlan gives a broad perspective on spiritual warfare and the deliverance process.

Schouppe, S.J., F. X. *Purgatory: Explained by the Lives and Legends of the Saints.* Rockford, IL: TAN Books, 1973.

This book gives a broad and detailed perspective on the souls in purgatory and the reality of their interaction with the living. One is taught the great value and need for praying for the dead. It has the Nihil Obstat and Imprimatur.